Grand Canyon

GRAND CANYON

A Visitor's Companion

George Wuerthner

Photographs by George Wuerthner
Illustrations by Douglas W. Moore

STACKPOLE
BOOKS

Published by
STACKPOLE BOOKS
5067 Ritter Road
Mechanicsburg, PA 17055

10 9 8 7 6 5 4 3 2 1

First edition

Printed in Hong Kong

Library of Congress Cataloging-in-Publication Data

Wuerthner, George.
    Grand Canyon : a visitor's companion / George Wuerthner ;
  photographs by George Wuerthner ; illustrations by Douglas W. Moore.
      p.   cm.
    Includes index.
    ISBN 0-8117-2492-1 (alk. paper)
    1. Grand Canyon National Park (Ariz.)—Guidebooks. 2. Grand
Canyon Region (Ariz.)—Guidebooks. I. Title.
F788.W93   1998
917.91'320453—dc21
                                                 97-30420
                                                  CIP

CONTENTS

About the Author

George Wuerthner is a full-time freelance photographer, writer, and ecologist. He has written nineteen other titles including *Yellowstone: A Visitor's Companion, Yosemite: A Visitor's Companion, Alaska Mountain Ranges, Forever Wild: The Adirondacks, Big Bend Country, Southern Appalachian Country, Montana: Magnificent Wilderness, Idaho Mountain Ranges, Nevada Mountain Ranges, Oregon Mountain Ranges,* and *The Maine Coast.* In addition, his photos have appeared in hundreds of calendars, books, magazines, and other publications. He has also exhibited at the Smithsonian Institution and other museums.

Wuerthner graduated from the University of Montana with degrees in wildlife biology and botany and received a master's degree in science communication from the University of California, Santa Cruz. A former wilderness ranger, national park ranger, botanist, science teacher, university instructor, and guide, Wuerthner now lives in Livingston, Montana, north of Yellowstone National Park.

INTRODUCTION

The Grand Canyon is one of the most impressive gorges on earth. Because of its extraordinary features, it has been designated a national park and the United Nations has listed it as a World Heritage Site.

No other canyon on earth rivals it, yet the flat approach across wooded plateaus gives no hint that the world is about to fall away in such spectacular fashion. But once at the edge, few are not moved by the vista. From the rim, the mighty Colorado River almost seems lost in the void. Indeed, the first Spanish to see the canyon could not conceive of its size and thought the river was not more than six feet across. After spending several days to reach the river, they realized their error. It's not that the Colorado is a tiny stream; it's that the canyon is so big.

My introduction to the canyon came during my sophomore year of college. For spring break, I hitchhiked from Montana to Grand Canyon National Park. Arriving on the South Rim toward sunset, I didn't have time to hike into the canyon immediately as I had hoped. I wandered along the rim a few miles from Grand Canyon Village looking for a place to sleep. I found a small level spot on the very lip of the canyon. Less than two feet from where my head lay, the world fell away thousands of feet. In the clear, starry sky, I could still make out the form of the canyon. Though years of scaling mountains has since ameliorated my fear of heights somewhat, I still don't like dangling my legs over the edges of bridges or cliffs. All night, I tossed and turned, worried I might roll over the rim. Watching the sun rise the next morning from the warmth of my sleeping bag made up for the restless night. Though I spent the next few weeks hiking the canyon backcountry, nothing surpassed that first starry night and sunrise from the canyon's rim.

As vast as the view was from my perch on the rim my first morning in the park, it encompassed only a small portion of the canyon. It is almost

Sunrise from Yaki Point, South Rim. The Grand Canyon is up to 18 miles wide and more than 280 miles long.

beyond comprehension—more than 280 miles long, up to 18 miles wide, and averaging 4,000 to 6,000 feet deep. Most of the canyon is protected as part of the national park, with a small portion of the western edge within Lake Mead National Recreation Area. Another fifteen miles upstream from Lees Ferry to Glen Canyon Dam is part of Glen Canyon National Recreational Area. So 292 miles of the river are within some land management unit, the longest protected stretch of canyon in the world and one of the largest protected river corridors as well.

Ecological Diversity

The park protects more than vistas or river corridors. It is one of the most ecologically diverse areas in North America. Within the park are a number of major ecosystem types, including the Sonoran, Mojave, and Great Basin deserts; Great Basin sagebrush; Great Basin pinyon-juniper woodland; and Rocky Mountain conifer forests. There also are six natural research areas covering 8,845 acres in the park. There are at least 1,500 plant species known in the park as well as 290 bird species, 90 species of mammals, 60 reptile and amphibian species, and 25 fish species. Seven animals are listed as endangered.

Management Responsibilities

Most of the central portion of the canyon is managed by the National Park Service. The park protects 1.2 million acres of the main canyon and adjacent rims. This is about half the size of Yellowstone National Park. National parks are managed differently from other federal lands, usually stressing nonconsumptive uses and natural landscape protection over exploitation. Logging, grazing, hunting, trapping, mining, and off-road vehicle use are usually not permitted.

Other parts of the canyon region are managed by the U.S. Forest Service and Bureau of Land Management. Both protect public resources but permit commercial activities that are commonly banned in national parks. On the east, the park is bordered by the Navajo Indian Reservation, while the Havasupai and Hualapai reservations border the canyon on the south and western reaches of the river. These are, in effect, large private landholdings held in trust by the tribes. Access, as on any private lands, is restricted. Indeed, beyond National Canyon and all the way to Grand Wash Cliffs, the lands adjacent to the south side of the Colorado River corridor aren't even in the park but are part of the Hualapai reservation.

Geographic and Geological Orientation

There isn't a single road crossing from the Navajo Bridge (which crosses the canyon by Marble Canyon) to Hoover Dam, a distance of more than 300 miles. The only other canyon crossing is the horse and hiker suspension bridge at Bright Angel Creek by Phantom Ranch. As most visitors can tell you, it's a long way around by road from the North Rim to the South Rim. Though a few maintained trails enter the canyon near Grand

Canyon Village, most of it is trailless. It is perhaps one of the most isolated wilderness tracts left in the United States outside of Alaska.

The park is in northern Arizona on the southwest corner of the Colorado Plateau Province, a huge region dominated by strata of sedimentary rocks. Water running over these rock layers for tens of thousands of years has cut deep gorges, canyons, buttes, mesas, and rims that make up some of the most spectacular scenery in the country. Numerous other national parks protect different segments of this region, including Canyonlands, Arches, Bryce, Zion, Capitol Reef, and Glen Canyon.

The Colorado River begins on the western slope of Colorado's Front Range, flows 1,440 miles across the Southwest, and empties into the Gulf of California in Mexico. Tributaries include the Green, San Juan, Yampa, Dolores, Gunnison, and White rivers. The Colorado and its tributaries drain seven states, with most of the flow coming from its headwaters and upper tributaries. Its lower reaches are arid, with little water being added to the river by the time it reaches the Grand Canyon.

Immediately adjacent to the river are a number of subsections to the Grand Canyon, beginning with Marble Canyon immediately below Lees Ferry. It is about 2,000 feet deep and relatively narrow, no more than four miles wide. Marble Canyon extends westward for about fifty miles to

Deer Creek drainage from Thunder River Trail.

Sunset at Marble Canyon. Marble Canyon is usually considered the beginning of the Grand Canyon.

Nankoweap Creek. Here it broadens out, assuming more magnificent proportions. Just beyond the confluence of the Little Colorado and Colorado rivers, the main part of the canyon officially begins.

Bordering the canyon on the south is the Coconino Plateau. It begins near Desert View and extends seventy-five miles west to Diamond Creek on the Hualapai reservation. This is locally known as the South Rim, which reaches its highest elevation, about 7,500 feet, by Grandview Point.

The north side of the canyon is broken up into four plateaus marked by major geological faults. From east to west, they are the Kaibab, Kanab, Uinkaret, and Shivwits. The Kaibab, known as the North Rim, has its lowest point at Cape Royal (7,865 feet), while its highest elevations are just shy of 9,200 feet. Only a portion of the Kaibab Plateau is within Grand Canyon National Park. The remainder is under forest service management in the Kaibab National Forest.

The general slope of the sedimentary layers of both rims is tilted toward the south, so the North Rim is about 1,000 feet higher than the South. The intervening rock has been eroded by the river. In addition, since more precipitation falls on the higher North Rim and the general tilt of

Ponderosa pine frames the volcanic San Francisco Peaks on the Coconino national Forest south of the Grand Canyon.

the land causes water to flow southward toward the Colorado River, the north side of the canyon has far more tributary streams and deeper side canyons.

Economic Value

The Grand Canyon is one of the chief visitor attractions in northern Arizona. In 1994, nearly 5 million people came to the park. By 2010, an estimated 6.8 million people will visit the park annually, spending $697.5 million in the region. Currently, 4,420 jobs in Coconino County, Arizona, are attributed to Grand Canyon visitation. This is expected to rise to 11,343 by 2010. During this same time period (1993–2010), visitors will pump $8.3 billion into the local economy.

Sweeping birds-eye view of the flat-topped forested surface of the Kaibab Plateau.

Despite the current hoopla about "loving our parks to death," most use is concentrated in a small part of most parks. The overall environmental impacts are minimal. Indeed, the Grand Canyon, along with adjoining federal and private holdings, represents one of the largest intact desert wilderness ecosystems left in North America. Despite the millions of people that may descend upon the South Rim overlooks annually, most of the canyon is nearly devoid of human imprint of any kind. When parking lots at the more popular scenic vistas are jammed, the canyon itself remains almost inaccessible. The park service is working on a plan to address the congestion and guide park management into the next century.

Elevation Chart

Here are the elevations of significant locations in the park and surrounding areas of interest. All elevations are in feet.

Location	Elevation
SOUTH RIM	
El Tovar Hotel	6,920
Mather Point	7,120
South entrance station	6,750
Hermit's Rest	6,640
Grandview Point	7,400
Desert View	7,500
Bright Angel trailhead	6,850
South Kaibab trailhead	7,200
NORTH RIM	
North Rim entrance station	8,830
North Rim lookout tower	9,165
Grand Canyon Lodge	8,200
North Rim ranger station	8,340
Point Imperial	8,800
Cape Royal	7,865
North Kaibab trailhead	8,240

Location	Elevation
OTHER PARK LOCATIONS	
Toroweap Campground	4,450
Tuweep ranger station	4,700
Phantom Ranch	2,400
Indian Garden	3,800
Roaring Springs	5,000
GRAND CANYON REGION	
Jacob Lake	8,150
Cameron	4,300
Flagstaff	7,000
Williams	6,700
Mount Humphreys (the highest point in Arizona)	12,635

CLIMATE

Packing clothes for a visit to the Grand Canyon is easy. Bring everything from a down coat to a swimsuit. Depending upon the weather on the river or high up on the North Rim, you might wear any of these items in a single day.

Weather at the Grand Canyon has a lot to do with elevation and slope. I've often started hiking amid snowdrifts on the South Rim at 7,000 feet and ended up wearing shorts and T-shirt when I reached the bottom of the canyon at 2,400 feet. Going down into the canyon is like traveling hundreds of miles to the south, but here the climatic changes are compressed into a few miles.

The climate of the Grand Canyon is similar to the rest of the Southwest: clear night skies, low humidity, moderate precipitation, gentle winter rains or snowfall, and violent summer thunderstorms. Nevertheless, every generalization must be qualified by where you happen to be in the park. It is colder and wetter the higher you go. Also, even at the same elevation, it is generally drier by Lake Mead at the western end of the canyon than by Marble Canyon in the east.

At 8,000 to 9,000 feet, the North Rim receives the greatest precipitation, often exceeding thirty inches a year, and experiences the lowest temperatures. On the other hand, the canyon bottom (at nearly 2,500 feet elevation) is the hottest and driest part of the park, averaging ten inches or less annually. During the drought of 1968, Phantom Ranch in the Inner Gorge near Bright Angel Creek received four inches of precipitation.

The high elevations on both rims also get a lot of snow. On the North Rim, average annual snowfall exceeds 120 inches. This is one reason North Rim roads are closed from November through May. The lower South Rim seldom gets more than a few inches of snow; what does fall typically melts within a few days.

The weather cycle is influenced by the canyon's location. The Grand Canyon lies at about the same latitude as other regions with relatively moderate climates, like Tennessee and North Africa. The canyon's generally sunny weather has much to do with its position at about thirty degrees north of the equator. Worldwide, this region is characterized by arid conditions resulting from descending air typically found at this latitude. Descending air warms, which allows it to absorb more moisture. The result is dry, sunny conditions.

The canyon's weather is also influenced by prevailing winds. Most of the year, air masses move into northern Arizona from the west. To reach Arizona, they must cross ranges such as the Sierra Nevada and other highlands in Southern California and Nevada. In rising over these mountains, the air is cooled and moisture falls out. By the time these air masses reach the Grand Canyon, much of the moisture has been wrung out of them.

The exception occurs in summer, when warm, moist air from the Gulf of Mexico is drawn up into the Southwest. Humid air often develops into towering thunderheads by late afternoon that lash the canyon with lightning, thunder, and downpours. By evening, most of the clouds dissipate, bringing clear night skies. These summer thunderstorms are responsible for much of the annual precipitation in the canyon. July and August are the wettest months for both the South Rim and the canyon bottom.

Winter and summer storms differ. Most winter storms produce steady, gentle rains or snow, whereas the summer storms tend to be dramatic, often deluging the canyon. Most flash flooding occurs during the summer.

Since summer thunderstorms often bring cloudy weather, if only temporarily, the high-summer months of July and August are not the sunniest times of the year. The clearest months are June and October. Temperaturewise, these are often the most pleasant times to visit either rim. However, be warned that by June, the inner canyon is already unbearably hot.

Weather also influences visibility at the canyon. In summer, prevailing winds bring in air pollutants from Southern California, Arizona, and New Mexico. The haze often dims the vivid colors of the canyon. In winter, winds come from more northerly, less polluted regions, improving visibility. In addition, winter cold fronts bring clear weather that enhances the crystalline nature of Grand Canyon vistas. Nevertheless, even in winter, the canyon occasionally suffers from air pollution. The winter pollution sources are more local, generally attributed to the nearby coal-fired Navajo Power Plant near Page, Arizona.

Compared with other regions of the country, such as the humid eastern states, the Grand Canyon experiences tremendous daily temperature fluctuations. In humid climates, heat is captured and held in the moist air. This is why Deep South summers are typified by hot, sticky days and unbearably warm nights. In the dry western air, temperature differences are often extreme. Even after a hot day, a lot of radiant energy is lost to the clear night sky, resulting in cool, pleasurable nights.

Summer temperatures tend to average more than 100 degrees in the canyon's inner gorge, while the higher elevations of the Kaibab Plateau experience average temperatures of 70 degrees or so. Nevertheless, temperatures of more than 115 degrees have been recorded in the Inner Gorge, which, combined with the dark rocks there, creates almost oven-like conditions. Heat stress is a major problem for hikers in summer.

Heat stress is not a problem in winter, although frostbite might be. Daytime winter temperatures average in the thirties and forties for the South Rim, but occasional arctic cold fronts can drop temperatures to zero or lower.

The rim of the canyon may be cloaked in snow and cold while the bottom, along the Colorado River, may be warm and springlike.

Weather Records

SOUTH RIM

Record low, –22° F.		Record high, 98° F.	
	Averages		
	High	**Low**	**Precipitation**
January	41° F.	18° F.	1.46 inches
February	45° F.	21° F.	1.63 inches
March	51° F.	25° F.	1.35 inches
April	60° F.	32° F.	0.87 inches
May	70° F.	39° F.	0.65 inches
June	81° F.	46° F.	0.39 inches
July	84° F.	54° F.	1.94 inches
August	81° F.	53° F.	2.32 inches
September	76° F.	47° F.	1.60 inches
October	65° F.	36° F.	1.18 inches
November	52° F.	27° F.	0.91 inches
December	43° F.	20° F.	1.69 inches

NORTH RIM

	Averages		
	High	**Low**	**Precipitation**
January	37° F.	16° F	3.17 inches
February	39° F.	18° F.	3.22 inches
March	44° F.	21° F.	2.63 inches
April	53° F.	29° F.	1.73 inches
May	62° F.	34° F.	1.17 inches
June	73° F.	40° F.	0.83 inches
July	77° F.	46° F.	1.93 inches
August	75° F.	45° F.	2.85 inches
September	69° F.	39° F.	1.99 inches
October	59° F.	31° F.	1.38 inches
November	46° F.	24° F.	1.48 inches
December	40° F.	20° F.	2.83 inches

INNER GORGE

	Averages		
	High	Low	Precipitation
January	56° F.	36° F.	0.68 inches
February	62° F.	42° F.	0.75 inches
March	71° F.	48° F.	0.79 inches
April	82° F.	56° F.	0.47 inches
May	92° F.	63° F.	0.36 inches
June	101° F.	72° F.	0.30 inches
July	106° F.	78° F.	0.84 inches
August	103° F.	75° F.	1.40 inches
September	97° F.	69° F.	0.97 inches
October	84° F.	58° F.	0.65 inches
November	68° F.	46° F.	0.43 inches
December	57° F.	37° F.	0.87 inches

Average Annual Climate Statistics from Selected Sites

Ranger station	Precipitation (inches)	Snowfall (inches)	Temp. range (low to high)	Frost-free days
NORTH RIM RANGER STATION				
8,340 feet	23.0	125.0	−25° to 91° F.	101
GRAND CANYON VILLAGE				
6,970 feet	14.5	65.0	−16° to 98° F.	148
TUWEEP RANGER STATION				
4,760 feet	11.7	9.2	0° to 108° F.	273
PHANTOM RANCH				
2,560 feet	8.5	0.2	−9° to 120° F.	331

HISTORY

First Immigrants

The Grand Canyon's history follows that of the entire Southwest. Many people have had encounters with the canyon, some positive and some less so, in part reflecting cultural perspectives and needs. There has been no one people strongly associated with the canyon for thousands of years. Indeed, even among Indians, there were long periods of time when, as far as can be determined, no humans lived in or near the canyon at all.

Archeological studies show humans have periodically settled the Grand Canyon, but no one resided in the canyon except during favorable climatic periods, when growing populations elsewhere forced people to use the marginal habitat there. Some people may simply have moved there because a favorable climatic period permitted humans to exploit the canyon. Whatever the explanation, wave after wave of different peoples have encountered the region, and the relatively recent arrival of Europeans is just the latest chapter.

The first immigrants to the Grand Canyon area were ancestors of today's Indian people. However, because of continual movements, the Indian groups near the Grand Canyon now are not thought to be direct descendants of earlier residents. The Navajo, for example, moved south from Canada to the canyon region about the same time as the advent of European exploration and settlement.

The first record of humans in the Southwest dates to about 9500 to 9000 B.C. These people, known as Paleo-Indians, hunted woolly mammoths, camels, and other large grazing animals that flourished in the region at the close of the last ice age. The Paleo-Indians went through several technological periods and eventually disappeared from the region, likely because of the extinction of their main prey.

About 7000 B.C. the Southwest was settled by a people less dependent upon big game for food. Known as the Archaic cultural tradition, these people used a greater variety of resources than the Paleo-Indians, supplementing their diet with plants and small game. The Archaic people left behind evidence of habitation within the canyon dating from 4,000 to 5,000 years ago. Within the canyon itself, tiny animal-like figurines from at least 2000 B.C. have been found. They may have been designed to bring hunting luck or for magic. No further evidence of these people exists and perhaps the canyon was again abandoned.

Approximately 2,000 years ago, a new cultural tradition invaded the Southwest from Mexico. Social organization and farming practices originating in Mexico spread north from Chihuahua and were adopted by the people of the Grand Canyon region. This included the cultivation of corn and squash. Gradually other crops, including beans, were domesticated and became part of the regional diet. At first, these early attempts at agriculture probably involved nothing more than planting some seeds and coming back to harvest whatever grew. It was not until about 500 B.C. that dependency upon agriculture led to more permanent residences.

The earliest of these agriculturists were the Anasazi, the Navajo name for "ancient ones." The first Anasazi to live in the Grand Canyon region were known as the "Basket Makers," for the twisted grass and yucca baskets they produced. They lived in northern Arizona between the first century and 700 A.D., or around the early Middle Ages in Europe. Even then, people and ideas were moving long distances about North America. These people had extensive trading ties, possessing shells, for example, from as far away as the Pacific. Farming did not replace the need for hunting and gathering of wild foods.

Around 700 A.D., the Basket Makers and their primitive pit houses were replaced by the Pueblo people. The term *pueblo* is Spanish for "town" and was applied to the numerous stone ruins and houses built by these people throughout the Southwest. They built towns of some size, housing several thousand people.

Like the Basket Makers, the Pueblo people grew corn as well as other crops, including cotton. They also made sophisticated pottery. Like earlier innovations such as farming, many of the cultural traditions (including much of the mythology, art, and ceremonies) of the Pueblo people reflected strong ties to Mexico. So did trade items, including macaw feathers, live birds, copper bells, and other artifacts.

Between 700 and 1000 (as Greenland was being colonized by Vikings), the Anasazi neared their peak in population and geographic distribution.

Marginal areas such as the Grand Canyon were colonized. Both rims of the canyon were settled, with small houses, irrigation ditches, and other developments. Between 1000 and 1100 A.D. (about the time William the Conqueror was invading England), these people reached their maximum population and distribution. Throughout the canyon country, they constructed numerous houses and granaries, and developed fields and irrigation systems. Typically, ruins are located in side canyons where there are permanent springs or streams. The longer growing season inside the canyon, coupled with available water, likely made the inner canyon attractive for settlement.

The Pueblo culture expansion marks the greatest human habitation of the canyon in history, up to and including today. A few settlements were even constructed on the North Rim; which due to the cool temperatures found at these high elevations, represents the upper limits to Indian agricultural production.

Suddenly, between 1150 and 1200, the entire Anasazi culture crashed. The Grand Canyon region was nearly abandoned, as were most of the larger pueblo towns to the north. The abandonment was different for each area; it was more rapid in marginal areas like the Grand Canyon, slower elsewhere. The ruins at Tusayan on the South Rim represent one of the last inhabited areas at the canyon. It was occupied in 1185 for about twenty years by about thirty people. A few other outposts like the large pueblo at Mesa Verde in southwestern Colorado hung on for another 100 years, but eventually it too was abandoned.

At about the same time the Anasazi were living in the canyon, another group, the Cohonina, moved into the region from the west. The Cohonina adopted many of the traditions of the Anasazi, including the construction of permanent houses, pottery making, and farming. Though water is much more scarce on the rims than inside the canyons, the Cohonina were able to colonize the rim plateaus because of a several hundred year period of increased precipitation across the region. They farmed along washes and other streams on the Coconino Plateau. Although they lived along the South Rim, their settlements never penetrated into the canyon itself, nor did they cross the Colorado to the North Rim. One reason for this may be that Pueblo people already occupied the best sites in these areas. The Cohonina disappeared from the region about the same time as the Pueblo people.

No one knows for certain why these people abandoned their settlements. Population increase in an already sparse environment may have led

Ruins at Tusayan on the South Rim. During a wet period around 1100 A.D., ancient Indian farmers were able to grow corn and other crops on the canyon rim. A prolonged drought that began around 1150 A.D. led to the abandonment of pueblo settlements in the entire Grand Canyon region.

to a depletion of resources. For example, wood may have been exhausted in areas of dense settlement. At Chaco Canyon, as many as 200,000 trees were cut for roof beams alone. Deforestation and accelerated soil erosion may have led to crop failure or drops in the water table. Toward the end of this period of social disorganization, nomadic hunters invaded the region. They competed for some of the same limited resources, such as wild game, and may have also raided the pueblo settlements. In the last quarter of the thirteenth century, a great drought spread across the Southwest, resulting in crop failures, completing the rout.

The life of these people was difficult. They suffered from many ailments. The lack of chimneys resulted in smoke-filled dwellings that contributed to respiratory problems. Skeletal remains show that degenerative arthritis, impacted teeth, and pyorrhea were common. By the time many of these people were in their thirties, the consumption of coarse stone-ground flour had worn their teeth down to the dentine. And there were always crop failures and a constant threat of warfare from other tribes.

By 1300 and continuing through the 1600s, nearly all descendants of the Pueblo people had resettled along the Rio Grande River in New Mexico or by permanent springs and waterways in northeast Arizona. We know their descendants as the Hopi and Pueblo tribes that still occupy the Four Corners region. Although the Grand Canyon was abandoned by the Pueblo people, some Hopis continued to visit the region, including the Little Colorado River drainage, where they sought out salt from natural outcrops.

At about this time or shortly after, the Paiutes, Navajos, and Apaches invaded the Southwest. The Paiutes occupied southern Nevada, southwestern Utah, and northwestern Arizona. The Navajos were more centered on the Four Corners. None of these tribes chose to live in the canyon, though their territories did sometimes extend to the rims. During this period, the Grand Canyon was essentially uninhabited.

However, as early as 1300, the Havasupai, a Yuman-speaking group from the Colorado River area near the California-Arizona line, began to move into the southwest corner of the Grand Canyon region. Eventually, they occupied Havasu Canyon, which drains into the western portion of the canyon. They are one of several Indian tribes still living in the area today.

The Spanish Era of Exploration

Beginning in the early 1500s, the first Europeans began their exploration of North America. Within twenty years of conquering Mexico in 1521, the Spanish had moved rapidly north and reached the rim of the Grand Canyon, discovered the mouth of the Colorado, and had partially explored its lower reaches. Considering how difficult travel was in this remote region, such an accomplishment is remarkable. Long before Plymouth Rock or Jamestown were colonized, Spanish soldiers were standing on the rim of the canyon peering down at the Colorado River.

Spain was a major seafaring nation, with a growing colonial empire in the Americas. It was interested in two things—gold and silver to support its military expansion and political ambitions in Europe, and the salvation of souls. With the aid of the sword and the Bible, plus European diseases that devastated the Indians, Spain colonized much of the Americas.

Within a few years of establishing a base in central Mexico, expeditions were sent to other regions in search of new wealth. One of the persistent myths of the New World was the existence of great treasures in the

Seven Cities of Cibola. In 1540, the governor of Mexico dispatched Francisco Vasquez de Coronado (for which a national forest in Arizona is named) to search for the cities. He was expected to rendezvous with another group of Spaniards who were exploring the western coast of Mexico by boat. Three ships under Hernando de Alarcon sailed up the Sea of Cortez to the mouth of the Colorado River, which Alarcon ascended beyond the confluence of the Gila River, becoming the first European to explore a great river of the West. Finding further ascent difficult, Alarcon turned around, failing to make contact with Coronado.

After six months, Coronado and his men reached one of the Zuni villages near the present Arizona–New Mexico line. They were disappointed not to find a city of gold. In an attempt to salvage something from the expedition, Coronado sent out patrols into the surrounding countryside. One patrol of twelve men under Garcia Lopez de Cardenas went to examine a large river rumored by the Indians to lie to the northwest. With Indian guides, Cardenas traveled for twenty days through a largely waterless landscape and reached a region that he described as "elevated and full of low-twisted pines, very cold and lying open to the north." Most historians believe they had reached the Grand Canyon around Desert View on the South Rim.

Having no real appreciation of the scale of the canyon, the Spanish believed the tiny river they could see below was no more than six feet across, though the Indians insisted it was much larger. They spent three days searching for a way down into the canyon. Several young soldiers became the first white men to descend into the abyss. After hours of hiking, they had descended only about a third of the way to the river, so they returned to the rim. The men confirmed that the river was much larger than they had thought. Cardenas and his men were the first Europeans to view the Grand Canyon.

The next European to venture into the canyon region was a missionary, Francisco Tomas Garces. In 1775–76, Garces and his Indian guides explored the Colorado River from its mouth to its canyons. In June 1776, Garces followed an Indian trail into Havasu Canyon, where he found the Havasupai living in the canyon that they still call home. Garces marveled at their orchards and fields with their elaborate irrigation system. Even this early, the Havasupai had cattle and horses they had obtained from the Hopi, who had probably obtained them from the Spanish.

Garces spent five days with the Havasupai, then continued east toward

Colorado River seen from Desert View, South Rim. The first Spanish exploration party under command of Garcia Lopez de Cardenas came upon the canyon and the river near this site. The Spanish believed the tiny river below was no more than six feet across, though the Indians guiding them insisted it was much larger.

the Hopi villages, encountering the Grand Canyon along the way. He was astonished at its roughness and the "barrier which nature has fixed therein." Upon reaching the Hopi, who were not welcoming, he returned to the Havasupai, spent six more days among them, then went back down the Colorado.

Besides providing a glimpse of early Indian life in the canyon region, Garces was the first to use the name "Grand Canyon" and consistently referred to the "Rio Colorado" in his writings.

Soon afterward, another group of Spanish missionaries skirted the region. Father Silvestre Velez de Escalante (for whom the Escalante River in Utah is named), with Father Francisco Dominguez and eight others, left Santa Fe, New Mexico, in late July 1776 to try to find a northern route to the new missions in California. His route took him into western Colorado, along the base of the Uinta Mountains in Utah, and eventually to Utah Lake south of present-day Salt Lake City. Running out of food and time, the expedition decided to turn back to Santa Fe. It worked its way southeast across southern Utah and forded the Colorado River at a place now known as the Crossing of the Fathers upstream from Lees Ferry. Eventually, Escalante made it back to Santa Fe. His party had become the first non-Indians to explore southern Utah and the Colorado upstream from the Grand Canyon.

Anglo Exploration

It took the salvation of souls and mythical cities of gold to lure the Spanish into the Southwest, but it was profitable trade, specifically in furs, that enticed Anglo-Americans to explore the Colorado Plateau. By the early 1800s, Lewis and Clark and other early explorers had mapped the outlines of what was to become the western United States. By the 1820s, venturesome free traders or mountain men were scouring the West for furs. Although we tend to think of these men as solitary wanderers in the wilderness, most trappers of this era worked in teams, forming fur companies. Traveling in groups of 20 to 100 people, including Indian camp followers and sometimes even families, these roving trappers systematically exploited region after region in the West.

In 1824, one of these traders, William H. Ashley (for whom the Ashley National Forest in Utah is named) and six other men journeyed down the Green River. Beginning in Wyoming, near where Interstate 80 now cuts across the southwestern corner of the state, Ashley floated through Flaming Gorge and the Uinta Mountains, ending his whitewater adventure near present-day Vernal, Utah. Ashley put the upper Green River on the map.

In 1826, a mountain man originally from Missouri, James Ohio Pattie, and other Americans like "Old Bill" Williams (for whom Williams, Arizona, is named), were trapping on the lower Gila and Colorado rivers in Arizona, where they were robbed of their furs by Indians. The men abandoned the lower Colorado and worked their way eastward. Although the exact route is difficult to trace given the sparse description in Pattie's journals, the best authorities believe Pattie's party headed upstream and passed along the rim of the Grand Canyon. Pattie said his party came to a place "where the mountains shut in so close upon its shores" that they "were compelled to climb a mountain, and travel along the acclivity, the river still in sight, and at an immense depth below." No doubt other trappers passed by the canyon, but few wrote of their adventures.

This era faded in the late 1830s as stream after stream was trapped out, nearly leading to the extinction of the beaver. The demand for beaver fur, which was used primarily for hats, also had declined because of changing fashion.

The next Anglos to enter the canyon region were government surveying parties. In 1848, the Grand Canyon became U.S. territory in the aftermath of the Mexican War. In 1850, the Arizona and New Mexico territories were created. The government sent out a number of military expeditions to explore and report on the newly acquired territory.

In 1851, Captain Lorenzo Sitgreaves (for whom the Sitgreaves National Forest in Arizona is named) pioneered a wagon route from the Zuni pueblos to Fort Yuma on the Colorado River, passing south of the Grand Canyon. Between 1853 and 1856, Lieutenant Amiel Whipple (for whom the Whipple Mountains in California are named) traipsed across Arizona surveying a route for the Southern Pacific Railroad, again passing just south of the Grand Canyon.

That both of these men passed so close to the canyon and did not visit it, nor comment about it, is not strange. Unlike a mountain, the canyon gives no hint of its presence until one is standing on the rim. It is easy to walk twenty or thirty feet from the edge and not know a great abyss lies just out of sight.

The next government explorer did not skirt the canyon. In 1857, the War Department directed Lieutenant Joseph Ives to determine the navigability of the Colorado for steamboats. Ives and his men went up as far as the Black Canyon by present-day Lake Mead until increasingly shallow waters and sandbars halted them. Ives abandoned the boat and his party set out by land, exploring the river farther upstream. The men descended into the inner gorge of the Grand Canyon along Diamond and Havasu creeks, becoming one of the first American parties to explore the western portion of the canyon. Ives was impressed with the rugged beauty and described the "gigantic chasms" with "vast ruins" and spires "that seem to be tottering upon their bases."

Although romantically stirred by the sweep of the canyon, Ives also viewed it as an obstacle to travel and pragmatically concluded that "the region is, of course, altogether valueless." He couldn't have been more wrong when he predicted in his 1861 *Report upon the Colorado River of the West*, "Ours has been the first, and will doubtless be the last, party of whites to visit this profitless locality. It seems intended by nature that the Colorado River, along the greater portion of its lonely and majestic ways shall be forever unvisited and undisturbed."

But the Ives expedition had inspired others with different perspectives on the canyon's value. In the party was John Strong Newberry (for whom Newberry Crater National Monument in Oregon is named), a physician and scientist. He was fascinated with the Grand Canyon's geological history. He made the first sketch of the canyon's geological strata column and proclaimed the canyon the "most splendid exposure of stratified rocks that there is in the world." He also was the first scientist to determine that water erosion had created the canyon and its tributary gorges.

Military expeditions were not the only visitors. In 1847, Brigham Young and his party of Mormons arrived in Utah. They began to lay out the new religious and commercial empire of Deseret at the base of the Wasatch Range by the Great Salt Lake. By 1850, church members were spreading out to establish new outposts in other parts of the new "Zion," including tiny settlements in southern Utah, southern Nevada, and northern Arizona. Between 1850 and 1870, such communities as Las Vegas, Kanab, St. George, Lees Ferry, and Tuba City were settled.

To coordinate and maintain church authority over these settlements, Young appointed the venerable Jacob Hamblin (Jacob Lake on the Kaibab Plateau is named for him). The capable Hamblin explored much of southern Utah's canyon country, locating several important Colorado River crossings, including the sites of Lees Ferry and Pierce Ferry. In 1862, Hamblin left St. George, Utah, crossed the river below the Grand Wash Cliffs, then circled south of the canyon and visited the Hopi villages. He recrossed the river by Lees Ferry, traversed the Kaibab Plateau, and made his way back to St. George, becoming the first white man to circumnavigate the canyon.

In 1867, Mormon colonists in Callville, Nevada, near present-day Lake Mead, found a half-dead, starving, sunburned man tied to a wooden raft floating on the Colorado River. When revived, the man identified himself as James White, a prospector, most recently from Colorado. He didn't know where he was, nor where he had been, except that he had floated for days through a large canyon with huge rapids that had repeatedly upset his raft. Since his circumstances and descriptions could only fit the

Grand Canyon of the Colorado, many credit White with being the first person to float the canyon. He apparently had no idea of the significance of his accomplishment until years later. He was just thankful to be alive.

White's incredible journey began when he and two prospecting partners were ambushed by Indians near the confluence of the Colorado and the San Juan River in southern Utah. One of the men was killed. White and the other man escaped by building a raft of cottonwood logs and floating down the Colorado. Not knowing the country nor the river, they were unprepared for rapids. At the very first whitewater, White's partner was tossed from the raft and drowned. At that point, White lashed himself to the raft and continued his float. He didn't remember much except that he passed through rapid after rapid and often was caught for hours in swirling eddies. At night, he would lash his raft to the bank and sleep with it, afraid that if it floated off without him, he would be lost. White said his journey took fourteen days, traveling nearly day and night.

Skeptics find his story almost unbelievable. How could anyone survive the Colorado's rapids on a homemade raft? On the other hand, why would anyone starve, sunburn, and nearly drown himself so that he could claim to be the first person through the Grand Canyon, long before the days of whitewater daredevils?

John Wesley Powell

No name is more closely associated with the Grand Canyon and the Colorado River than John Wesley Powell. From Powell Point on the South Rim to the Powell Plateau on the North Rim to Lake Powell behind Glen Canyon Dam, Powell's name and accomplishments are memorialized. Although James White *may* have been the first person to negotiate the canyon and live to tell about it, most historians credit Powell with making the first successful (and verifiable) descent of the Colorado River. Powell is also credited with surveying the last major region of unexplored territory in the continental United States.

Powell was born in 1834 and grew up on the frontier in the Midwest. A voracious reader, he was largely self-taught. Although he did attend several colleges, he never earned a degree. During the Civil War, Powell was a Union Army officer and was wounded at the Battle of Shiloh in 1862, resulting in the amputation of his right arm.

After the war, Powell taught geology at Illinois Wesleyan University. In 1867 and 1868, Powell and his students and family undertook several field trips to the Rockies to study geology and Indians. The idea of running the Colorado River in order to investigate its geology apparently arose during these trips. By 1869, he had read all he could find about the river, including reviewing Ives's report. He had obtained some funding from several museums, his university, and the federal government to undertake an expedition down the river. Powell was joined by nine other men, including his brother and an assortment of other western adventurers, mostly former Union soldiers. The little group set off in four boats in May 1869 from Green River, Wyoming, which was by then accessible by the Union Pacific Railroad.

The boats had been built to Powell's design. Three of the double-ribbed oak craft were twenty-one feet long and weighed nearly a half-ton each. They had built-in watertight compartments for flotation and two rowing seats, one behind the other. The boats could carry up to 2,000 pounds of gear apiece. The fourth boat was smaller and lighter; Powell used it for scouting.

The green crew, with limited river-running experience, found the initial whitewater of the Green River exciting. Their excitement faded as the risk became apparent. Despite their solid construction, one of the boats was destroyed—a little more than two weeks into the trip—in Ledore Canyon on rapids now known as Disaster Falls. No one was hurt, but one of the party's members, Frank Goodman, was discouraged enough to leave the expedition near present-day Vernal, Utah.

After resupplying with food from the Unita Indian Reservation agency, the party continued down the river, ran Desolation Canyon, and arrived on July 17 at the confluence of the Grand (the former name for the Colorado) and Green rivers. By August 4, the party had run Cataract Canyon and passed the mouth of the Paria River near present-day Lees Ferry. By August 10, the men had passed through Marble Canyon and camped at the mouth of the Little Colorado River.

By then the men had become seasoned boatmen and had long abandoned any romantic notions about being on a grand vacation. They were almost constantly drenched. When they weren't, they were often baked by the afternoon heat of the canyon. Night winds frequently whipped sand into their faces as they attempted to sleep. Nights without wind were worse, as hordes of mosquitoes attacked the sleeping men. Their clothes and shoes were ripped unavoidably by shrubs, boulders, and weather.

One journal makes the point. Just beyond Bright Angel Creek, Powell notes: "It is especially cold in the rain tonight. The little canvas we have is rotten and useless; the rubber ponchos, with which we started from Green River City, have all been lost; more than half the party is without hats, and not one of us has an entire suit of clothes, and we have not a blanket apiece. So we gather drift wood and build a fire; but after supper the rain, coming down in torrents, extinguishes it, and we sit up all night on the rocks, shivering, and are more exhausted by the night's discomfort than by the day's toil."

Running the endless unknown rapids extracted its toll as well. One of the boats had swamped, tossing Powell and two others into the river. The boats, battered by rocks and boulders, needed unending repair, and new oars had to be made from driftwood to replace continually splintered ones.

After losing one boat in Ledore Canyon, the party seldom risked another upset in the rapids. The men couldn't afford to lose any more provisions. Most of the larger drops were "lined," rather than run. Ropes were attached fore and aft and the heavy boats dropped down the river along the bank, guided by the men, who were slipping and sliding in the mud or taking tumbles on mossy boulders. Sometimes lining was impossible. The boats were then unloaded and the heavy craft portaged by rolling them on driftwood logs. If portage was impossible, the unloaded vessels were run down empty. No matter how it was done, every run of rapids required some risk, hard labor, and anxiety.

By the time they reached Granite Gorge, their provisions were getting short. They had little beyond flour, coffee, and dried apples. The canyon rose to new heights and the rapids and rocks continued to batter the boats. The men were largely in unknown territory, with only the sketchi-est notion of what was ahead. Powell described this reach of the canyon as "grand, gloomy depths." He registered his growing apprehension: "We have an unknown distance yet to run; an unknown river yet to explore. What falls there are, we know not; what rocks beset the channel, we know not; what walls rise over the river, we know not. Ah well! We may con-jecture many things. The men talk as cheerfully as ever; jests are bandied about freely this morning; but to me the cheer is somber and the jests ghastly."

In his diary, George Bradley, one of Powell's men, reported a different perspective of the crew's mood. "The men are uneasy and discontented and eager to move on. If the Major does not do something soon I fear the consequences, but he is contented and seems to think that biscuit made of sour and musty flour and a few dried apples is ample to sustain a laboring man."

On August 27, they came to a place where side canyons on either bank of the river had dumped boulders into the river. With cliffs blocking any chance for a portage, the expedition had no choice but to run what was judged to be the worst rapids encountered so far. The continual strain led three members—Bill Dunn, Oramil Howell, and his brother, Seneca—to declare that any further advance would be suicidal. They decided to climb out of the canyon and work their way north toward the southern Utah Mormon settlements. At a place now known as Separation Rapid, the men were given a portion of the remaining food, rifles, and ammunition, and they began to climb out of the canyon. Before they could reach the settlements, however, they were killed by Paiute Indians.

The expedition, now down to two boats and six men, ran the last few rapids, including Lava Cliff. A mishap there almost cost the men the expedition. In attempting to line around the rapids, the stern post pulled out on a boat to which the rope was attached, sending the craft containing George Bradley down into the maelstrom. Powell, Billy Hawkins, and Andy Hall pursued in the second boat. Powell's brother traveled on shore. He was then taken aboard a boat. Miraculously, Bradley guided his boat safely down the giant waves to the foot of the rapids. Powell's boat was upset in the giant troughs, throwing all three men into the rapids. Bradley scooped them out once they reached the calmer water.

After that, the two boats and crews ran the rest of the river in less than a day and passed out of the canyon by the Grand Wash Cliffs. They were the first men acknowledged to have documented a run through the Grand Canyon.

At the mouth of the Virgin River, Powell and his brother left the river. The remaining four continued down the Colorado to Fort Yuma. Jack Sumner and Bradley called it quits there, but Hall and Hawkins proceeded all the way to the Gulf of California, becoming the first men known to have descended the Colorado from the Green River to its mouth in Mexico.

The success of this expedition prompted Congress to back another river trip. Powell immediately began making plans; this time he wanted to do a more thorough job of collecting scientific information. At the same time,

Powell was appointed director of the new Geographical and Geological Survey of the Rocky Mountain Region. In this capacity, he returned to the Grand Canyon region in the summer of 1870 to search for potential resupply points for the proposed second expedition. Guided by Jacob Hamblin, he explored the North Rim region, taking notes on its geology and Indians.

In 1871, Powell was back in Green River, Wyoming. This time, his crew consisted less of adventurers and more of scientists, plus a surveyor and a professional photographer. They set out on May 22. The expedition never seemed to click. Boats overturned and additional supplies went astray. Powell left the river for thirty-nine days to visit his pregnant wife in Salt Lake City. By October 23, they had reached Lees Ferry, where they halted for the winter. A number of the expedition members quit. Powell and his remaining crew spent much of the rest of 1871 and 1872 exploring the region north of the Grand Canyon, including the Kaibab Plateau.

It was not until August 17, 1872, that the river trip was resumed. The river seemed higher than on Powell's previous journey. Below Bright Angel Creek, the surging water flipped Powell's boat. By the time he reached Kanab Creek on September 8, enthusiasm for finishing the trip was ebbing. There they met a packer with supplies who told of rising tensions among the Indians. That seemed to convince Powell; he terminated his second trip at Kanab Creek, only halfway through the canyon.

When Powell later wrote the official account of his 1869 trip, he incorporated some of the events and place names from his second trip without ever mentioning it or crediting any of its members. This led to some ill will between Powell and his comrades.

Though he did not completely run the canyon a second time, Powell had made worthy accomplishments. He became the second director of the U.S. Geological Survey and founder and first director of the Bureau of American Ethnology. Realizing that the arid West had limited capacity for settlement and that nearly all human activities would be focused on areas with water, Powell recommended changing the homesteading and other laws to reflect these realities. This caused friction among many western boosters, who thought his ideas would restrict settlement. For these ideas and others, he was eventually forced from government service.

Nevertheless, Powell was involved in Grand Canyon surveys and expeditions for decades. During a field trip to the North Rim in 1882–83, his party constructed the Nankoweap Trail, which drops from the eastern edge of the Kaibab Plateau to the river just upstream from the confluence of the Little Colorado River. In 1891, Powell and other geologists organized a trip to the canyon for the International Congress of Geologists.

Other Surveys

Powell's explorations were not the only government-sponsored surveys of the Grand Canyon. At the same time as the second Powell expedition, a government party under Lieutenant George M. Wheeler, a surveyor, was working its way up the Colorado River. Like Powell's second Grand Canyon party, Wheeler's survey included some professional men, including seven scientists and a photographer, plus six boatman, six soldiers, and more than a dozen Mojave Indians. The expedition members wrestled their boats up through Lava Cliff Rapids and Separation Rapid to Diamond Creek in the western Grand Canyon. At this point, some of the men walked out. The others descended back through the very rapids that had nearly ended the first Powell expedition in 1869.

Despite the laborious ascent, Wheeler still managed to appreciate the grandeur of his surroundings and anticipated their tourist attraction: "[The canyons of the Colorado] stand without a rival upon the face of the globe, must always remain one of the wonders, and will, as circumstances of transportation permit, attract the denizens of all quarters of the world who in their travels delight to gaze upon the intricacies of nature."

In 1880, another geological expedition was launched by Clarence Dutton, a protégé of Powell's who had accompanied him on a survey to the region in 1875. A widely read intellectual with a romantic flair, Dutton spent fifteen field seasons teasing apart the geological history of the Colorado Plateau. His first monograph, "Geology of the High Plateaus of Utah," explored the geological formation of the Giant Stairstep of plateaus that descends from southern Utah to the Colorado River.

Next he turned to the Grand Canyon, exploring its northern boundaries, including the Tonoweap Valley and Kaibab Plateau. These surveys resulted in another important geological report, "The Tertiary History of the Grand Canyon District, with Atlas." Dutton was taken with the Grand Canyon's beauty as much as its geology. With lyrical descriptions that seemed so out of place for a scientist, Dutton described the canyon's ever-changing moods. To the romantic Dutton, the great rocky spires and mesas resembled great temples. In keeping with this spirit, he named many of the canyon's features for religious figures and mythology: Shiva Temple, Vishnu Temple, Brahma Temple, and the Tower of Babel.

The next major survey of the river wasn't for science but commerce. In 1889–90, Robert Brewster Stanton, an engineer, was hired to survey the Grand Canyon as a potential railroad route from Colorado to California. Stanton ran the river twice, suffering setbacks and tragedies. The first river journey started in Green River, Wyoming, but several deaths, including the drowning of Frank Brown, the railroad president, ended the trip partway through the Grand Canyon. His second trip began in December 1889 and was also filled with trouble, including the near death of one party member, who fell from the cliffs. Despite these problems, Stanton's second expedition traversed the entire canyon and made it to Mexico, the second group to negotiate the Colorado from the Green River to the gulf. Stanton made a detailed report and recommendations, but the railroad was never built. He didn't fade away, however, later setting up a gold-dredge mining operation in Glen Canyon.

After Stanton, only two other parties ran the Colorado before the turn of the century. None of these men were survey or scientific experts; they were in for the adventure.

The first group consisted of George Flavell, an adventurer and trapper, and a young Mexican, Ramon Montez. In a homemade boat, the pair left Green River on April 27, 1896. Unlike earlier boatmen, Flavell pointed his bow upstream. With the stern facing downstream, he could easily watch for rocks and waves. Instead of rowing furiously through rapids as earlier canyon runners had done, Flavell only gave occasional sweeps of his oars when it was necessary to pull away from a dangerous place—his method has been used by river runners ever since.

Early in their trip, Flavell and Montez found it was difficult for two men to line a boat down rapids. After a few attempts at this, they largely abandoned lining and portaging, finding it easier just to run the rapids. So, instead of avoiding most of the whitewater, Flavell and Montez ran nearly everything. Dispensing with the tedious tasks of portaging and lining, the pair ran the Grand Canyon from Lees Ferry to Grand Wash Cliffs in just thirteen days. They continued downstream, with Montez dropping out at Needles, California, while Flavell went all the way to Yuma, Arizona.

Just behind Flavell and Montez were Nathaniel Galloway and William Richmond. Ostensibly, the two were floating the Colorado to trap furs and check out the mining prospects. In October 1896, they set out from Desolation Canyon on the Green and floated leisurely, arriving in Needles on February 10, 1897. In 1909, Galloway ran the river again, becoming the first person to run it twice through its entire length.

First Settlers

While Powell, Dutton, Wheeler, and Stanton were putting the Grand Canyon on the map, others were being drawn to the region. Mormon settlement expanded and traffic across the Colorado River between southern Utah and northern Arizona increased sufficiently to support a ferry just upstream from Marble Canyon. It is now known as Lees Ferry, established in 1871 by John Doyle Lee. Lee was executed in 1877 for participating in the Mountain Meadows massacre, in which non-Mormon pioneers were killed by Mormons. His wife continued to operate the ferry until the Mormon Church purchased it from her in 1879. The ferry operated under a variety of owners until 1928, when the Navajo Bridge opened at Marble Canyon. Today Lees Ferry is usually the start of most float trips through the Grand Canyon. It also is the official separation between the lower and upper Colorado River Basin.

Besides setting up a rudimentary transportation network, the Mormons also began to exploit the natural resources of the canyon country. Timber for buildings was often obtained from the higher forested areas like Mount Trumbull and the Kaibab Plateau. The first sawmill on the Kaibab opened at Big Springs in 1871, the year of Powell's second trip.

At about the same time, herds of sheep and cattle were being driven up into the same country. As early as 1877, southern Utah stockmen were wintering animals in the House Rock Valley and summering them on the pastures on the Kaibab Plateau. By the 1880s and 1890s, most of the range was controlled by large cattle companies.

Railroads and Tourist Trade

The Grand Canyon might have remained an interesting, perhaps inspiring, backdrop for stockmen and lumberjacks had it not been for the publicity generated by Powell, Dutton, and other scientists attracted to the canyon. The tourist era began with the completion of a railroad across northern Arizona. By 1882, railroad lines had spawned the communities of Flagstaff, Williams, and Peach Springs. The last, twenty-five miles from the South Rim, was closest to the canyon.

By 1884, the first hotel in the Grand Canyon area was constructed. Tourists arrrived at Peach Springs by train, then proceeded by stage and horseback down Peach Spring Wash and Diamond Creek to the Colorado River opposite Shivwits Plateau in the western Grand Canyon. It is still possible to make this trek, which is now through part of the Hualapai reservation.

Peach Springs was soon surpassed as a tourist jumping-off point by Ash Fork, Williams, and Flagstaff. Roads were built from these communities to the South Rim; stage lines provided transport from the rail stations to hotels and camps near the canyon. By 1892, it was a one-day journey by stage from Flagstaff to the South Rim. The fare was $20.

The residents of Flagstaff began working for a spur line to the canyon during the 1880s and 1890s. In 1898, a mining company with claims near the South Rim began to lay tracks from Williams south to the rim. When the mining venture failed, the railroad, nearly completed, was sold to the Santa Fe railway, which completed the track to the South Rim near present-day Grand Canyon Village in 1901. Tourism in the canyon rapidly increased.

Prospectors and Grand Canyon Trails

Wandering throughout the canyon country were prospectors, always searching for the next El Dorado. Numerous claims were staked in the canyon and a few mines operated over the years. Silver, gold, lead, copper, asbestos, and uranium have all been found in the canyon, but few deposits were worth the expense of development in such rugged terrain. The Mormons operated a copper mine near Jacob Lake on the Kaibab Plateau. Copper-mining districts also were opened by Mount Trumbull and Grand Wash Cliffs. The ever-optimistic miners were among the first whites to explore the nooks and crannies of the canyon away from the river.

A few of these miners found they could collect more gold from the pockets of tourists than from the canyon's recesses. In fact, nearly all of the early trails that are still used, including the Bass, Tanner, Bright Angel, Hermit, Hance, and Grandview, were originally constructed and maintained by prospectors–turned–tour guides.

One of the first was John Hance, who arrived at the canyon in 1883. He built a trail that still bears his name from the South Rim near Moran Point to some asbestos claims he had staked by the river. Within a few years, Hance was spending more time entertaining guests and guiding

Hiker at Grandview Point. Grandview Point was the site of John Hance's lodge, built in 1886. It was one of the first tourist accommodations on the canyon rim.

mule trips into the canyon than he was on mining. He built a hotel by Grandview Point and by 1886 was advertising his services in the Flagstaff newspapers. His reputation as a teller of fanciful and colorful adventures kept guests coming back year after year. Hance died in 1919 and is buried in a local cemetery.

In the same mold was Wallace Bass. A prospector who became a guide and hotelier, Bass arrived in Williams in 1883. By 1890, he had built a road from Williams to Havasu Canyon. Eventually, he operated a stage-coach that ferried tourists between town and the canyon, where he had a rustic resort known as Bass Camp. Then he linked some old Indian and prospector trails down Bass Canyon to the river at Bass Rapids. In time, he established a ferry on the river and built the North Bass Trail up Shinumo Creek. Along the creek, Bass built another guest camp and maintained a garden and orchard. Bass's system was the first cross-canyon trail passable by horse constructed in the Grand Canyon.

During the off-season, Bass continued to prospect. He actually oper-ated a small copper mine in Copper Canyon, but the difficulty of getting the ore out precluded significant development.

The most easterly of these old prospector trails is the Tanner Trail, named for Seth Tanner. He explored much of the eastern Grand Canyon in the pursuit of minerals and developed a small copper deposit near the Colorado River. Tanner improved an old Indian trail from Lipan Point to Tanner Canyon Rapids, where it connects to the river trail that runs all the way to the Little Colorado River confluence.

The Hermit Trail commemorates another prospector and tour guide, the French-Canadian Louis Boucher. He had a base camp at Dripping Springs. Later, he built a few rude cabins for tourists on a copper claim farther down Boucher Canyon.

The best-known trail in the Grand Canyon is the Bright Angel. It runs from the South Rim near the present Grand Canyon Village, down a series of switchbacks to Indian Gardens on the Tonto Plateau. From here it is possible to continue to the Colorado River, then cross the river on a bridge to Phantom Ranch and reach the North Rim via the North Kaibab Trail.

Like other trails on the South Rim, the Bright Angel was pioneered by brothers Niles and Ralph Cameron, and Pete Berry, all prospectors who became tourism promoters. Cameron, Arizona, to the east of the Grand Canyon, is named for Ralph. In 1890, the three men widened an old Indian trail to get to mining claims they hoped to develop in the canyon. However, within a few years, it was evident that tourism was more prof-itable. By 1903, Ralph Cameron had bought out the other two and begun to charge $1 a person for use of the trail.

To consolidate his holdings, Cameron exploited an 1872 mining law

Cottonwood trees at Indian Gardens and the Tonto Plateau seen along the Bright Angel Trail. Use of the Bright Angel Trail led to one of the earliest controversies in the park. Ralph Cameron, miner and early advocate of using public resources for private gain, battled the Park Service over his "claims" to ownership of the Bright Angel Trail.

that allows anyone to file claims to mineral deposits or suspected deposits on unappropriated public lands. Cameron soon had more than 13,000 acres in the canyon tied up with mining claims at strategic points along his trail, controlling the greatest trail mileage possible. In addition, he sought claims to several sites on the top of the South Rim as well as at Indian Gardens. (This antiquated law is still on the books, though some in Congress are attempting to reform it to reflect 1990s realities.)

Cameron's claims were an obvious attempt to control tourism development on the South Rim. Cameron's claims were challenged by many, including the federal government and the Santa Fe railroad, which planned to construct a lodge on the rim.

But Cameron had a great deal of local support. He was elected chairman of the Coconino County Board of Supervisors in 1904. Shortly afterward, ownership of the trail passed to the county. However, the county decided it could not afford to maintain the trail and leased it to L. L.

Ferrell, who continued to collect fees. This was just a diversionary tactic, since Cameron was maneuvering to get back the lucrative operation.

Cameron went to the state legislature in Phoenix and got what was known as the Cameron Bill passed. It was vetoed by the governor but upheld by both houses of the legislature. The bill allowed the county to enter into a contract with anyone to operate a toll road. Upon passage of the Cameron Bill, the Santa Fe railroad immediately offered to take over operations of the trail and return 70 percent of the tolls to the county. But Coconino County officials had other ideas. They brazenly awarded the toll trail contract to Ralph Cameron. Under the contract, Cameron got to keep 90 percent of the money.

In 1919, Cameron filed fifty-five new mining claims in the canyon. In 1920, after years of litigation, including review by the U.S. Supreme Court, all of his claims were invalidated, largely because they contained no real mineral value, as required by the mining law. Just as the National Park Service was about to force Cameron's compliance with the court ruling, he was elected to the U.S. Senate. Once in office, Cameron immediately got supporters appointed as a federal judge, U.S. attorney, and U.S. marshal, and was able to stall enforcement of the Supreme Court decision for a number of years. For these and other shenanigans, Cameron was publicly denounced on the floor of the House of Representatives, but this only enraged the senator more. To get back at the park service and its supporters in Congress, Cameron temporarily blocked the yearly appropriation for Grand Canyon National Park operations. Launching a new attack and vindictive to the end, Cameron set up a congressional committee to "investigate" park operations, where he unceasingly attacked park service management.

Despite gross actions of self-interest, Cameron maintained support by capitalizing on local animosity toward the federal government and large corporations. He portrayed his land grab and other efforts to thwart the park service as a case of the "little guy" fighting big government and big business. Nevertheless, Cameron eventually wore out his support even in Arizona and was defeated for reelection.

After Grand Canyon National Park was created in 1919, the federal government became involved in negotiations for the trail. Due to hard feelings generated locally over the creation of the national park, the county refused to cooperate. Eventually, however, a bill was passed in the state legislature that more or less ordered the county to sell the trail to the federal government. In 1928, the issue was laid to rest when the federal government agreed to pay $1 million for the trail (which was originally federal property anyway), with the funds being used to help construct a highway to the South Rim.

As might have been expected, Ralph Cameron fought the sale to the bitter end, arguing that the federal government had to maintain an approach road to the park anyway and the sale of the trail shouldn't be tied to the road construction.

While the debate over Bright Angel Trail raged, the Santa Fe railroad built its own trail to the bottom of the canyon so as to avoid Cameron's operations. Beginning in 1912, the railroad constructed a road out to Hermit's Rest, now known as West Rim Drive. From there, it built the Hermit Trail, paving it with sandstone blocks in some sections. A rest house was built at Santa Maria Springs, and Hermit Camp, an overnight facility, was constructed on the Tonto Plateau. Visitors arrived by mule, but supplies were delivered by a tram from Pima Point. By 1916, there was even phone service at the camp. The camp was closed in 1930 and most of the buildings were removed, but the foundations are still visible from the rim at Pima Point.

The dominance of railroad transportation was first challenged in 1902 by the automobile. The Toledo Eight Horse, a steam-driven vehicle, left Flagstaff on January 4 for the Grand Canyon. It was trouble prone and it took five days for the adventurers to reach the South Rim. By 1926, cars had eclipsed railroads as the preferred means of travel to the park.

Formation of the Park

As the explorations of Powell, Dutton, and others became known in the late 1880s and '90s, national pride in the Grand Canyon grew. Europe had its cathedrals, but America had scenic wonders. Yellowstone National Park, established in 1872 as the world's first national park, created a national precedent for protecting scenic landscapes and geological wonders from development and individual greed.

Keep in mind the prevailing attitude of the era. The federal government was doing just about everything it could to give away the public domain. The Homestead Act, passed in 1864, permitted anyone to claim up to 160 acres of unreserved public land for farming. Other acts of Congress such as the Timber and Stone Act encouraged individuals to claim and develop public lands throughout the West. Hundreds of millions of acres were given away to the railroads to encourage their expansion.

Particularly prevalent on the frontier was the view that any undeveloped and unexploited lands were a waste—indeed, almost anti-Christian and ungodly. The notion of making any landscapes off-limits to private ownership was a major shift in thinking.

Some argue, however, that the motivation for national parks was not entirely without commercial interest. One of the early supporters of a Grand Canyon national park was the railroad, since it stood to gain significantly from a major tourist attraction.

That the creation of a national park was influenced by avarice does not diminish the event's significance. The idea of protecting part of the landscape as a park was a recognition of limitations, that completely unregulated and uncontrolled exploitation was not always in the nation's long-term interest. Acting upon these more altruistic motives, Senator Benjamin Harrison proposed the establishment of a Grand Canyon national park as early as 1886. The proposal went nowhere, but the idea was not dead.

After Harrison was elected president in 1888, he revived the idea. In 1891, Congress authorized the president to create forest reserves. Two years later, Harrison used executive privilege to designate fifteen reserves, including an area surrounding the Grand Canyon. These lands were withdrawn from settlement as part of the Great Canyon Reserve. The move was not entirely welcomed by local inhabitants, who viewed the restrictions on mining, logging, grazing, and settlement as a threat to their "right" to use the public domain freely. In 1898, the Coconino County Board of Supervisors officially proclaimed its opposition and requested that all lands be immediately opened to settlement and other exploitation.

John Muir, founder of the Sierra Club and one of the most prominent spokesmen for the natural world at the turn of the century, wrote an article in 1898 for the *Atlantic Monthly* in which he wrote of the Grand Canyon: "So incomparably lovely and grand and supreme it is above all the other canyons in our fire-molded, earthquake-shaken, rain-washed, wave-washed, river and glacier sculptured world." Muir ended his article by calling for the creation of a Grand Canyon national park.

In 1903, the canyon came closer to park status when President Theodore Roosevelt visited the South Rim. Roosevelt, a staunch conservationist, was enchanted with the canyon, stating that it was the "most impressive piece of scenery I have ever looked at." In a speech before hundreds of Arizonans, the president reflected upon the abyss. "In the Grand Canyon, Arizona has a natural wonder which, so far as I know, is in kind absolutely unparalleled throughout the rest of the world. I want to ask you to do one thing in connection with it in your own interest and in the interest of the country—to keep this great wonder of nature as it is now. . . . I hope you will not have a building of any kind, not a summer cottage, a hotel or anything else, to mar the wonderful grandeur, the sublimity, the great loveliness and beauty of the Canyon. Leave it as it is. You can not improve on it. The ages have been at work upon it, and man can only mar it. What you can do is to keep it for your children, your children's children, and for all who come after you, as one of the great sights which every American if he can travel at all should."

In 1906, Roosevelt signed a bill that created a Grand Canyon game reserve, though in keeping with the perspective of the day, this protection did not extend to predators. In 1905, the U.S. Forest Service was established, and in 1907, the Grand Canyon area was placed within the Grand Canyon National Forest. National forest designation only withdrew public domain lands from settlement. It did not restrict commercial or private use and exploitation of these lands. Unlike national parks, national forests were open to hunting, grazing, logging, and mining. Though an ardent hunter, Roosevelt believed that national park status was more appropriate for the Grand Canyon, but only Congress can declare a park, so he could not change the status of lands surrounding the canyon.

In 1906, however, Congress gave Roosevelt an unexpected opportunity when it passed the Act for the Preservation of American Antiquities. This law permitted the president to designate lands that had "objects of historic or scientific interest" as "national monuments." The law likely was designed to enable the president to set aside small areas like Indian ruins. But Roosevelt took a broad interpretation of the law and reasoned that the entire Grand Canyon had scientific and historic value. On January 11, 1908, Roosevelt declared the central portion of the Grand Canyon a national monument. Many people living near the canyon and used to having unrestricted access to public resources were outraged. The proclamation was challenged, but eventually Roosevent's authority and interpretation of the law were upheld by the Supreme Court.

With the establishment of the Grand Canyon National Monument, the former Grand Canyon National Forest was split in two. The south half became part of the Coconino National Forest and the north portion was designated the Kaibab National Forest.

Arizona achieved statehood in 1912 and the movement to create a national park gained momentum. The National Park Service was estab-

Sunset at Mather Point. The Grand Canyon was first set aside as a national monument by President Theodore Roosevelt by executive order in 1907.

lished in 1916 to run the growing list of parks throughout the country. Congress directed the park service to "conserve the scenery and the natural and historic objects and the wildlife therein and to provide for the enjoyment of the same in such manner and by such means as will leave them unimpaired for the enjoyment of future generations."

Local opposition remained strong—especially among stockmen—but in other parts of Arizona, there was a growing interest in the establishment of a national park to promote tourism.

In effort to create a tourist draw while nullifying much of the protection provided by Roosevelt's proclamation, a bill was introduced by Arizonans in Congress in 1917. It sought to create a national park that was significantly smaller than the existing national monument. In further appeasement of local interests, it also permitted mineral exploration and development within the proposed park. And it removed from the boundaries of the existing national monument most of the timberlands of the Kaibab Plateau and grazing lands on both sides of the canyon.

Sunset afterglow seen at Moran Point. Moran Point is named for the great landscape painter Thomas Moran, who helped to promote national parks through his paintings.

Although the bill did create a national park, it actually weakened protection of the area and reduced its size. With a push from the Arizona delegation, the bill passed both houses of Congress, and President Woodrow Wilson signed it on February 26, 1919, making the Grand Canyon the seventeenth national park.

But opposition to the park idea was weakening. In 1927, Congress, with the support of Arizona Senator Carl Hayden, rectified some of the deficiencies in the earlier park bill by expanding the boundaries of the Grand Canyon to include more of the Kaibab Plateau, bringing the total acreage to 645,760. New mining claims were prohibited in 1931. In 1932, President Herbert Hoover invoked the Antiquities Act again to declare a new Grand Canyon National Monument, setting aside 273,145 acres to the west of the national park to protect additional reaches of the canyon. In

1940, a portion of this expanded national monument was excluded by executive order of President Franklin Roosevelt, again shrinking the area protected under park service management.

Despite this setback, efforts to protect more of the canyon continued. In 1969, another presidential proclamation established Marble Canyon National Monument. In 1975, the Grand Canyon Enlargement Act combined Marble Canyon National Monument with the old Grand Canyon National Monument lands left after the retrenchment of 1940, so that a larger continuous national park of 1,216,000 acres stretched from Grand Wash Cliffs to the Paria River. The current park covers an area roughly half the size of Yellowstone and slightly more than a third of the size of Death Valley National Park.

Dams

In the arid West, water determines everything. From the crude irrigation networks of the Anasazi to the increasing sophistication of Mormon irrigation projects to the present, water development has gone hand in hand with settlement and, especially, agriculture. Not only is western precipitation sparse, but it is less reliable and more variable than in areas farther east. Providing a reliable source of water has been a focus of efforts in the region for a long time.

The modern solution has been the construction of taxpayer-supported reclamation projects. In 1922, Arizona, Utah, Colorado, Wyoming, California, Nevada, and New Mexico—all with claims to the Colorado River and its tributaries—created the Colorado River Compact. It divided the river basin into upper and lower sections at Lees Ferry and allotted the river's flow among the states. There was extensive bickering over the terms. Arizona refused to sign, so the document eventually was ratified as a six-state compact. After additional congressional wrangling, a bill passed providing for several dams on the Colorado as well as aqueducts to carry water to farms and cities.

The bill authorized Boulder Dam (now Hoover Dam) on the Colorado River near Las Vegas, Nevada. It was the largest in the world when completed. No matter what you may think of the dam today, it was unsurpassed as an engineering feat in its day, being 726 feet tall, 1,244 feet long, and 660 feet thick at its base.

Thousands of depression-era workers swarmed to the site looking for employment, and work began on May 12, 1931. First the river had to be diverted. Four fifty-foot tunnels were blasted through bedrock, some more than three-quarters of a mile long. The tunnels took eighteen months, and when the entire flow of the river was diverted, workers immediately began building the wooden forms to hold the concrete that would fill the river channel. A plant was constructed that could produce 6,600 yards of concrete every twenty-four hours. Railroad cars carried buckets of the wet concrete to the dam site, where cranes hoisted them skyward and dumped them into the forms. For twenty-two months, the concrete buckets were emptied, one every minute. The dam was largely finished by 1935 and dedicated by President Franklin Roosevelt. It took six years for the river to fill the reservoir—Lake Mead—behind the dam. It stretches 110 miles upstream, flooding the lower 43 miles of the Grand Canyon. Lake Mead is now managed as a national recreation area, providing many water sports opportunities.

Despite Lake Mead's effect on the lower portion of the Grand Canyon, the largest impact upon the canyon came with the completion of Glen Canyon Dam in 1963. It was authorized by Congress in 1956 as part of the Colorado River Storage Project Act. The law led to the construction of three other dams: Flaming Gorge on the Green River in Wyoming, the Curecanti on the Gunnison in Colorado, and the Navajo on the San Juan in New Mexico. Glen Canyon, the lowest on the upper-river system, was built largely to store water in the upper Colorado River basin for the use of Arizona and Utah and to supplement downstream use.

The Glen Canyon Dam was an alternative to a proposal to dam the Yampa River at Echo Park within Dinosaur National Monument. The idea of flooding a national monument (and a spectacular canyon) was odious to environmentalists. Led by the Sierra Club, opponents got the dam removed from the Colorado River Storage legislation. It was the first time that a major dam project had been rejected in favor of preserving a wild river. But in winning the Echo Park controversy, conservationists lost the equally enchanting Glen Canyon, appreciated too late as the "Place No One Knew."

Glen Canyon Dam is now the money machine for the Colorado River Storage Project Act, generating millions of dollars from the sale of hydroelectric power. It produces about 70 percent of the hydroelectric power in the intermountain West, serving nearly 2 million people. Though taxpayers paid for the dam, the power isn't free. Ratepayers' money is used to subsidize irrigation benefiting farmers and ranchers elsewhere in the

Colorado River basin, who often produce crops and animals that are already raised in abundance elsewhere without irrigation.

Never calculated in the original consideration were the environmental costs to the river. Once the floodgates were closed, the water created Lake Powell, one of the largest reservoirs in North America. Most of this area is now managed by the National Park Service as part of Glen Canyon National Recreation Area. This has radically altered the preexisting wild river.

The flow peaks and lows are controlled, with fewer floods. This is leading to the loss of sandy beaches in the canyon. The water flow varies daily as well, following the needs for hydroelectric production. The water below the dam is also much colder and clearer, changing the environment for aquatic species. Native fish, adapted to the undammed Colorado's higher temperatures and sediments, have been displaced by exotic species.

Glen Canyon was not the last dam proposal for the Colorado River. For decades, two sites within the Grand Canyon itself had been eyed by engineers—Bridge Creek on the lower Grand Canyon and Marble Canyon just below Lees Ferry. In 1963, the Bureau of Reclamation proposed construction of these dams. These two hydroelectric projects would pay for the construction of an aqueduct from Lake Havasu on the lower Colorado River to the rapidly growing urban areas of Tucson and Phoenix as part of the Central Arizona Project. The dams were supported by Interior Secretary Stewart Udall as well as many in Congress. Their construction was considered almost a done deal.

Yet, environmentalists were not ready to lose the last free-flowing parts of the Colorado River and part of the Grand Canyon so easily. On June 9, 1966, a full-page ad placed by the Sierra Club in the *Washington Post* and *New York Times* declared, "Now Only You Can Save Grand Canyon from Being Flooded—for Profit." Stung, dam supporters in Congress managed to get the Internal Revenue Service on June 10 to threaten to revoke the Sierra Club's nonprofit status for trying to influence legislation. Eventually, the club did lose nonprofit status. In the meantime, even people who didn't care much about the Grand Canyon were mobilized against the dams by the publicity. A flood of letters soon hit Congress.

In response, the Bureau of Reclamation claimed that its Bridge Canyon dam wouldn't hurt the scenic qualities of the Grand Canyon and the resulting lake would make it easier for tourists to see the river. The Sierra Club fought back with another ad that asked: "Should we also flood the

Sistine Chapel so tourists can get nearer the ceiling?" The environmentalists argued that there were other ways to fund a water delivery project.

Dam supporters in Congress came back with a new proposal. They would abandon the Marble Canyon dam and extend the park upstream to include the Marble Canyon area, but build the Bridge Canyon dam and abolish Grand Canyon National Monument so an officially designated part of the park would be affected.

The Sierra Club continued its opposition to any dam proposals and was branded as unreasonable and uncompromising, not unlike accusations made against environmentalists now. In congressional hearings, David Brower, executive director of the Sierra Club, argued that not only were the dams unnecessary, since alternative power sources were available, but there was no other Grand Canyon. Brower said he would not compromise what was irreplaceable, of global significance, and a national treasure to produce something that could be obtained better elsewhere. He said the issue was no different than if the Greeks wanted to level the Parthenon to build a parking lot.

Under Brower's leadership, opposition to any dams in the Grand Canyon grew to the point that in 1967, President Lyndon Johnson's administration withdrew its support. The Arizonans in Congress could not resurrect the dam projects and Congress passed a revised Central Arizona Project that did not include dams on either site. The legislation even specifically stated that no dams could ever be built in the Grand Canyon.

Today, the 277 miles of the Colorado River through the Grand Canyon form the longest stretch still in its natural condition and one of the longest navigable whitewater rivers left in the world. This segment easily qualifies for designation as a national wild and scenic river but, since the river is largely protected by being in a national park, no formal protection of the river has been proposed in Congress.

Ongoing Environmental Issues

Running the rapids of the Colorado, once the domain of a few adventurers, became a major industry when surplus army rubber rafts became available after World War II. In 1954, only 200 people had ever run through the canyon. By 1966, more than 1,000 people were floating down the river in a single season. By 1972, the number was 16,000 a year. The river corridor was no longer remote. Studies showed trampled vegetation, heavily used campsites, and litter. Competition for the best campsites was becoming keen.

Most of these effects were social or cosmetic, affecting visitor perceptions of "wilderness" rather than posing long-term environmental damage. Still, the park service felt it had to begin regulating river use to maintain some semblance of scenic beauty and an unharried experience for floaters.

In the early 1970s, all floaters were required to apply for a spot on the river. The system has not enjoyed the full support of all users. A lottery is held each winter, with only 15 percent of the permits going to the public. The rest are reserved for commercial outfitters. It takes an average of eight years for a private boater to get a permit to run the canyon. However, anyone willing to pay for a guided trip can go down the river as often as he likes, since commercial operators hold so many permits. Some argue that such a system not only is unjust, since wealthy people can easily afford numerous trips, but also privatizes a public resource.

Most critics do not object to the restriction on floaters, but they argue that permits should be allotted to individuals rather than outfitters. They say anyone interested in floating the river should be able to apply for a permit and, if he receives one, choose to go on his own or go with an outfitter. In essence, critics would like to see river use regulated like hunting, because hunters with permits can choose to use an outfitter or not.

River access is only one of many issues. There is increasing concern over congestion and crowding along the South Rim, particularly in summer. Visitation has increased from 44,000 in 1919 to 4.7 million in 1994. Some 820,000 day hikers walked partway down into the canyon in that same year, and there were another 108,800 backcountry "user nights" (a single person who stays five nights accounts for five user nights). During the peak month of July, more than 735,000 people visited the canyon in 1994!

In response, the park service has drafted a management plan that, among other things, proposes a staging area near Mather Point with a large parking lot from which people can ride buses or bicycles to other points along the rim. Development will be encouraged outside the park and historic buildings within the park will be adapted for other uses.

Another issue is scenic flights. The first airport was developed by Red Butte in the 1920s. A new one was constructed near Tusayan just south of the park in 1962 and traffic has increased. In 1993, more than 535,000 people deplaned at the Tusayan airport, making it the third-busiest in Arizona. These people and others on tours originating elsewhere, resulted in more than 820,000 people cruising over the canyon in either a helicopter or plane. Many people find air tours exciting and memorable, but people on the ground complain of the intrusion on their solitude. There is also concern that noise affects wildlife from bighorn sheep to peregrine falcons. The issue is unresolved.

If projections for visitation are accurate, greater restrictions may be needed. Still, do not assume that people are "loving the park to death." Nearly all human activity is concentrated on a small portion of the South Rim accessible by road. Most of the canyon is virtually untouched wilderness and will remain so.

Wilderness

More than a million acres of the Grand Canyon (or about 90 percent) is suitable for designation as wilderness, designed to protect landscapes against manipulation. Although the National Park Service manages most of the undeveloped portions of the Grand Canyon as wilderness, this is only an administrative designation that could change with any new park superintendent. Only Congress can give legal protection. In 1980, at the direction of Congress, a wilderness proposal was drafted by the park service. It was updated in 1993 and proposes designation of 1,109,257 acres as wilderness.

If Congress chooses to act, this area, with the adjacent designated and proposed 400,000 acres of wilderness on other public lands, would create the largest desert wilderness in the United States.

The Grand Canyon has many values, but perhaps its greatest is its national and global significance in cultural heritage. The canyon has assumed a cultural and religious status among Americans and others. In many ways, a journey to the Grand Canyon is to many Americans like a journey to Mecca might be for a Moslem or a visit to the Ganges River for a Hindu. It is a national religious shrine. While access should remain as unencumbered as possible, visitation and all development should be respectful to the canyon as well as to present and future generations. It is in this tradition that the National Park Service labors.

GEOLOGY

The Grand Canyon is first and foremost a geological wonder. It is neither the longest nor deepest canyon in the world, but few others expose such a continuous and extensive geological record. It has among the best preserved and exposed sedimentary rock sequences found in the world. In fact, President Theodore Roosevelt used its geological attributes to justify his declaration of the canyon as a national monument under the 1906 Antiquities Act.

The canyon was carved from the sedimentary formations of the Colorado Plateau, a huge area that encompasses the Four Corners region of southern Utah, southwestern Colorado, northwestern New Mexico, and northern Arizona. The bottom of the canyon is carved through hard metamorphic rocks nearly 2 billion years old, while the sedimentary and volcanic layers of rocks above are progressively younger. Beyond the canyon are even younger rocks, making up the stairstep of plateaus and cliffs that runs from the Boulder Mountain region of southern Utah south to the Colorado River, including the Pink, White, Vermillion, and Chocolate cliffs.

The canyon rim comprises six plateaus, all bounded by faults. To the south of the river lie the Coconino and Hualapai plateaus. To the north lie the Kaibab, Kanab, Uinkaret, and Shivwits plateaus. The eastern portion of the Kaibab Plateau is bounded by the East Kaibab Monocline, a major fault system that more or less defines the beginnings of the Grand Canyon.

The sedimentary layers found on the North Rim continue across the canyon to the South Rim. Erosion by the Colorado River has stripped away the intervening rock, but the structure on both rims is the same. Because of its slope, the North Rim is approximately 1,000 feet higher.

This slope also explains the canyon's hydrology. Most of the streams

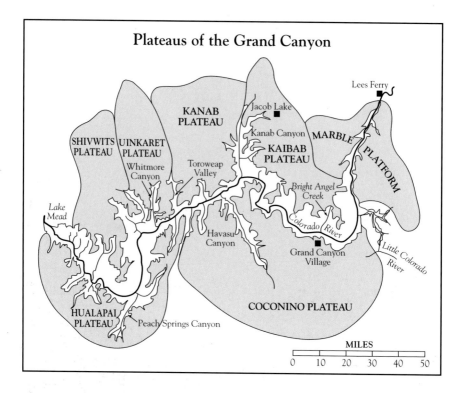

Plateaus of the Grand Canyon

entering it descend from the North Rim. Streams flowing down from plateaus on the north side of the river have much longer canyons as well. The reasons are related to geology. Since the North Rim is higher, it captures more snow and rain. It also slopes down toward the river, so water falling along the North Rim naturally flows toward the river. The South Rim, on the other hand, slopes away from the river, so water falling on the South Rim flows away from the river.

Before the construction of dams upstream at Glen Canyon and elsewhere, the Colorado River drainage basin was lowered 6½ inches every 1,000 years due to erosion. This produced astounding amounts of sediment. It was the abundance of sediment in the river that led John Wesley Powell to believe that waterfalls were unlikely in the canyon, as some expected, since the scouring power of sediment would cut through any resistant rock layers.

Nevertheless, there are plenty of rapids in the Grand Canyon. Nearly all are where tributaries enter the river. Since the gradient on tributaries is greater than on the river itself, during floods the streams can carry boulders into the river that are too big for the river to move. Debris and boulders washed into the river then partially block the channel. Although the river eventually erodes away these rocks, new flash floods continue to re-create the barrier. Thus the rapids remain in more or less the same locations year after year.

The position of these rapid-producing streams is largely controlled by

Most rapids on the Colorado like those seen here are formed by side canyons that pour rubble and boulders into the river during flash floods.

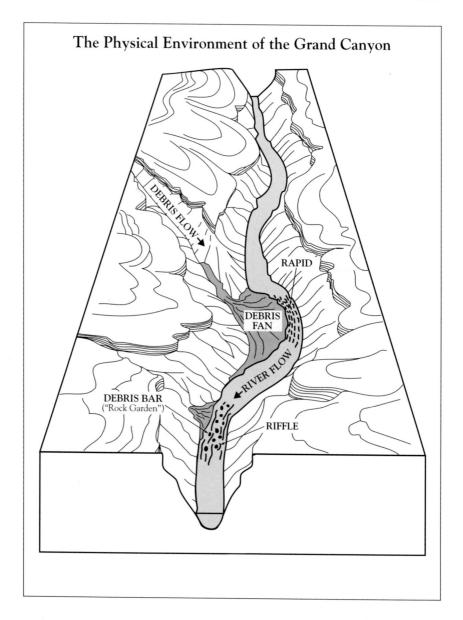

The Physical Environment of the Grand Canyon

DEBRIS FLOW

RAPID

DEBRIS FAN

RIVER FLOW

DEBRIS BAR
("Rock Garden")

RIFFLE

geological faults. These weaknesses in the rock are exploited by streams as channels. One can almost determine the location of rapids using a geological map that shows the position of faults crossing the river.

Though the size of the canyon gives the impression that it must have existed for millions of years, the Grand Canyon is surprisingly young. The canyon visible from the rim was carved in less than 2 million years.

Humans were well along their evolutionary path, so the canyon has existed no longer than humans have wandered the earth. When people talk about the great age of the canyon, they are talking about the rocks, not the canyon itself.

Geological Time Scale

The age of the planet is continually being pushed back, but the most recent estimates place it at 4.5 billion years or more. This vast time is divided up into eras, periods, and epochs. These time periods represent pivotal breaks in earth history, signaling either major extinctions or development of new life forms, or globally significant geological events such as the breakup of continental land masses.

The oldest geological time division in earth history is the Precambrian Era, which encompasses the first 3.9 billion years of the planet's development. Precambrian Era rocks are found in North America with some dated to nearly 4 billion years ago. Precambrian Era rocks are also found in the Inner Gorge of the Grand Canyon and are nearly 2 billion years old.

It was originally thought that no life existed during the Precambrian Era because there were no apparent fossils to document its existence. Recently, using new interpretations, it has been established that simple life forms like algae existed in the world's oceans for hundreds of millions of years.

Approximately 600 million years ago, the Precambrian Era was followed by the Paleozoic Era (meaning "old life"). This signals the beginning of very elemental forms of life that were first preserved and recognized as fossils. It was during the Paleozoic that the first fishes evolved. The next era is the Mesozoic Era ("middle life"), which lasted some 180 million years and was signaled by the development of reptiles, including the dinosaurs. The most recent division is the Cenozoic Era ("recent life"), which began approximately 60 million years ago and takes us up to the present. The evolution of mammals occurred primarily during the Cenozoic Era.

Each of these eras are further divided into periods and epochs. For example, the Mesozoic Era consists of three subunits: Triassic, Jurassic, and Cretaceous.

The names of periods and eras refer to the places where these kinds of rocks were first described. For instance, the Cretaceous age rocks refers to the limestone chalks of England, while the Jurassic name is derived from the Jura Mountains in France.

GEOLOGICAL TIME SCALE FOR THE GRAND CANYON

Rock formations	Years before present	Epoch	Period	Era
Volcanic rocks	10,000–present	Recent	Quaternary	Cenozoic
	2.5 million–10,000	Pleistocene		
	9–2.5 million	Pliocene	Tertiary	
	25–9 million	Miocene		
	40–25 million	Oligocene		
	60–40 million	Eocene		
	70–60 million	Paleocene		
No formations	135–70 million		Cretaceous	Mesozoic
No formations	180–135 million		Jurassic	
Rocks of Cedar Mountain and Red Butte	225–180 million		Triassic	

Rock formations	Age of formation in years	Period	Era
Kaibab Formation	250 million	Permian	Paleozoic
Toroweap Formation	255 million		
Coconino Sandstone	260 million		
Hermit Shale	265 million		
Supai Group	285 million	Pennsylvanian	
Redwall Limestone	335 million	Mississippian	
Temple Butte Limestone	350 million	Devonian	
No formations	500–400 million	Silurian & Ordovician	
Muav Limestone	515 million	Cambrian	
Bright Angel Shale	530 million		
Tapeats Sandstone	545 million		
Grand Canyon Supergroup	1.2 billion		Precambrian
Vishnu Schnist	2 billion		

Rock Types

Rocks are divided into three primary classes—sedimentary, igneous, and metamorphic—depending upon their origins. All are well represented in the Grand Canyon.

The most obvious Grand Canyon rocks are sedimentary, which make up most of the canyon walls. As the name implies, they are formed from sediment, the particles of rock that are dissolved in water or broken up by erosion, then deposited by water, wind, or glacial ice. Sedimentary rocks are formed on the earth's surface, though they may later be buried by new rock layers.

Sedimentary rocks are initially all bedded horizontally, although these layers may later be twisted or tilted. Since sediment is typically deposited layer by layer, the oldest rocks in a sequence are those buried the deepest. In the Grand Canyon, the oldest rocks are exposed at the bottom of the gorge, with progressively younger outcrops found as you approach the rims of the plateaus.

Well-known sedimentary rocks include sandstone, limestone, and shale. All three are prominent in the walls of the Grand Canyon. Sandstone is formed from particles of sand cemented together. Shale is formed from mud and silt. Limestone is created from limy mud or the cemented fragmented particles of shells of animals like clams.

Fossil water marks in sandstone.

Close-up of bedded sandstone formed as windborne sand dunes. This is a good example of the deposition one sees in sedimentary rocks.

Most of the cliffs exposed in the Grand Canyon are composed of sedimentary rocks of varying hardness and strength. Easily eroded sediments (such as shales) form gentle slopes, while well-cemented, harder rocks like limestones tend to form sheer cliffs. Such differing erosion gives rise to the stairstep formation of cliff and slope so obvious in the canyon.

Igneous rocks are produced from molten material deep in the earth. Sometimes it moves to the surface through volcanoes. Basalt, andesite, and rhyolite are all common igneous rocks. Recent volcanic activity is evident in the western Grand Canyon in the form of such features as Vulcans Throne and Lava Falls, created by lava flows.

Molten rock that cools and hardens in the earth is known as intrusive igneous rock. Granite is a common example. Bodies of granite are called plutons and a number are exposed in the Inner Gorge.

The last major rock type is metamorphic. This means "to change form." Metamorphic rocks are created from either sedimentary or igneous rocks and changed by heat and pressure into a new form. This usually occurs deep in the earth. The only opportunity to observe metamorphic rocks is when they are exposed at the surface by erosion. Marble is a well-known metamorphic rock created from recrystallized limestone. Gneiss is metamorphosed granite or sandstone. Schist is metamorphosed shale. The Vishnu Schists of the Inner Gorge are metamorphosed sedimentary and igneous rocks.

Plate Tectonics

The Grand Canyon's geological history is tied into a larger framework of continental movements. Just as the events that shaped the human history of the Grand Canyon are part of a larger human drama, the canyon's geological history makes sense only when placed within a context of planetary events. The prevailing theory that explains the larger phenomenon is known as plate tectonics.

This states that the earth's crust is broken in about a dozen large pieces and many smaller ones. The continents and ocean basins are all made up of individual plates or composites of several plates. Each of the continent-sized plate pieces has a central stable core called a craton. New material can be added around the cratons, enlarging them, or lost when a plate rifts apart or is overridden by another plate. All of these plates float on molten rock much as chunks of ice might float in a river. As the earth's magma circulates, it drags the plates across the planet's surface.

The North America plate was once joined to Europe. About 250 million years ago, it split off and began moving westward. The Atlantic Ocean basin opened in its wake. At this time, the leading edge of North America was somewhere east of the present-day Rockies. As the North American plate moved westward, island arcs and pieces of other minicontinental plates collided with it and were added onto the edge of the continent. Nearly all of the rocks that make up the Rockies and lands farther west originated elsewhere (moved by plate tectonics) and were welded to North America.

The Grand Canyon sits on one corner of the old plate margin. The rocks that make up most of the sedimentary rocks visible in the canyon were deposited on the edge of the growing continent, which at that time was near the tropics. Subsequently, this continental plate was moved several thousand miles northward and rotated at the same time.

Typically, ocean plates are heavier than continental plates. When the two meet, as they do along the western margin of North America, the oceanic plate dives under the continental plate. The forces created by plate collision provide the heat and pressure to metamorphose rocks and also are responsible for the faults or cracks in the earth's crust.

In the Grand Canyon region, north-south boundary faults mark the margins of all major plateaus. These faults, from west to east, are Grand Wash, Hurricane, Toroweap, West Kaibab, and the East Kaibab Monocline. They represent the southern extension of the regional faults responsible for the uplift of the Wasatch Mountains and many southern Utah plateaus.

Smaller faults also define most of the tributary canyons in the Grand Canyon. These creeks have cut their channels along fault-induced weaknesses in the rock strata. The long canyon of Bright Angel Creek and

The straight canyon of Bright Angel Creek seen in the center left portion of the photo follows the weakness in the earth's crust created by the Bright Angel Fault.

the route followed by the Bright Angel Trail on the South Rim trace the Bright Angel Fault, which runs from the North to the South Rim. Kanab Creek, another major tributary of the Colorado, also follows a major fault. The Grand Wash Cliffs, which mark the western edge of the Grand Canyon, also are bounded by faults.

Slippage associated with sliding plates also results in earthquakes. Since the western edge of North America is overriding the Pacific plate, there is a great deal of earthquake activity along the Pacific Coast, while the Midwest and East Coast are relatively stable. Although not as seismically active as California, the Colorado Plateau is close enough to the western edge of the continent to be affected by plate collisions. There have been at least forty-five earthquakes in the Grand Canyon region in this century. At least five have exceeded 5 on the Richter Scale, with the largest recent one at 5.75.

As the overridden edge of a plate moves deeper into the earth, it melts. Some of this molten rock rises toward the surface to erupt as a volcano. The line of volcanoes in the Cascades of Oregon and Washington marks the ongoing collision of the North American and Pacific plates. Not all volcanic activity is a marker of plate margins, however. Lava can erupt where fault stresses permit molten rock to reach the surface. Most of the recent volcanic activity in the Grand Canyon region is associated with such fault movement.

One of the unusual aspects of the Colorado Plateau is its geologic stability. Few parts of the world have remained so stable for so long. Measurements of the earth's crust beneath the Colorado Plateau suggests that it is thicker and the flow of heat less than in adjacent areas. It is believed that for much of its history, the seismically quiet Colorado Plateau lay at the trailing edge of a continent, similar to the position of today's eastern United States. This lack of significant faulting and other crust movement is one reason why the sedimentary layering of the Grand Canyon region has been preserved so well.

The breakup and collision of plates causes mountains to be raised, ocean basins to form, and seas to advance and retreat as new pieces are added or lost. At times, sediment is deposited in ocean basins. Then, with seismic uplifting, these sediments may rise above sea level to be exposed to erosion. The eroded surfaces may then be inundated again. This continual uplifting, erosion, and subsiding has given rise to the rock assemblages exposed in the Grand Canyon.

Geological History

Many of the rock formations in the canyon were named for nearby natural features. There is Tapeats Sandstone, named for Tapeats Creek, where this outcrop was first studied. The Kaibab Limestone is named for the Kaibab Plateau, which is capped by this rock. Hermit Shale is named for Hermit Creek, and so on.

The youngest exposed rocks are at the rim of the canyon; the oldest are at the bottom. Except for the Inner Gorge and the Grand Canyon Super-

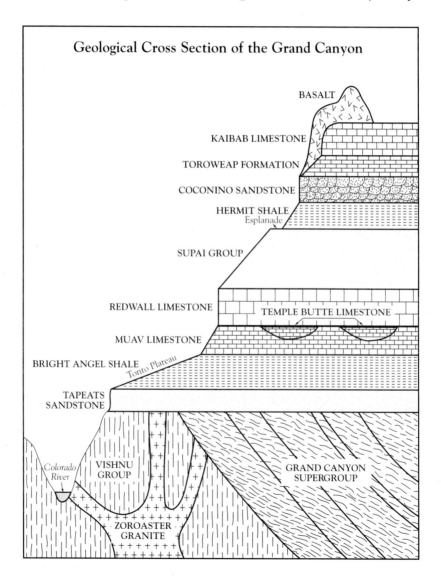

group rocks just above it, all the strata seen in the canyon developed 570 million to 250 million years ago. Since these are the most obvious rocks in the canyon (and of the most interest to tourists), learning the names of the major outcrops is useful. In descending order, the most obvious rocks are Kaibab Limestone, Toroweap Formation, Coconino Sandstone, Hermit Shale, Supai Group, Redwall Limestone, Muav Limestone, Bright Angel Shale, and Tapeats Sandstone. A good way to remember these rocks is to use the phrase "Know The Canyon's History, See Rocks Made By Time." Most of these major formations are divided into subgroups, each with its own name. These are for avid geology buffs only.

The easiest way to lay out the geological history is to begin with the oldest rocks and work up toward the rim. The lowest portions of the Grand Canyon are not readily seen from the rim but are composed of ancient metamorphic rocks that differ markedly from the overlying sedimentary layers that dominate the canyon.

Vishnu Metamorphic Complex

The oldest rocks exposed in the Grand Canyon, the Vishnu Schist and Zoroaster Granite, are in the Inner Gorge. They represent the early development of the southwestern edge of the North American plate. They were originally island arcs grafted onto the growing edge of North America. They are similar in age and composition to rocks exposed by erosion in the Black Canyon of the Gunnison River in Colorado.

The Vishnu Schist is named for the Hindu preserver of religion and was first described at Vishnu Creek. These schists began forming 2 billion years ago when sediment and volcanic ash were deposited in a shallow sea. Associated with the sediment are lava flows and ash layers.

The sediment and volcanic rocks were subjected to at least two metamorphic episodes. About 1.7 billion years ago, an ongoing collision of plates twice produced enough pressure and heat to metamorphose these sedimentary rocks into the Vishnu Schist. Schist is fine-grained rock of nearly uniform texture and appearance.

Around 1.5 billion years ago, injections of magma into the schist gave rise to the Zoroaster Granite that now makes up the Granite Gorge and other parts of the river canyon. About twenty small bodies of granite, plus dikes and sills, are scattered throughout the canyon. Zoroaster is named for the founder of the Zoroastrian religion, a precursor of Judaism and Christianity.

The Precambrian Vishnu Schist of the Inner Gorge. Schist is much harder rock than the overlying sedimentary formation, and therefore more difficult for the river to erode.

Grand Canyon Supergroup

Lying directly above the rocks of the Inner Gorge are very old sedimentary and slightly metamorphosed rock strata known as the Grand Canyon Supergroup. The Supergroup is easily distinguished from other rocks since it is the only major rock layer that is tilted off of horizontal. The Supergroup outcrop can be seen from many locations on the South Rim. The largest outcrop lies upstream from Hance Rapid in the eastern Grand Canyon across the Colorado River from Desert View on the South Rim.

The Supergroup is a thick deposit of tilted strata sandwiched between the crystalline rocks of the Inner Gorge and the younger, nearly horizontal sedimentary rocks above it. The Grand Canyon Supergroup is divided into several subsections known as the Unkar and Chuar groups, with the Nankoweap Formation lying in between the two.

It is important to recognize that the deposition of rock strata in the Grand Canyon is part of a larger regional geological process. Comparisons of the Grand Canyon Supergroup with other rocks in North America suggest that these sediments were likely formed during the same time as the rock strata found in Montana's Glacier National Park and the McKenzie Mountains of the Northwest Territories in Canada.

The Supergroup was laid down between 1.25 billion and 1.07 billion years ago. These largely sedimentary rocks have been slightly metamorphosed but retain much of their original horizontal appearance. They consist of mudstones, limestones, shales, quartzites, and lava flows. Ripple marks and desiccation cracks preserved in some of these sediments suggest that many were on the edge of a shallow sea while others seem to have been deposited in deeper water.

The entire Supergroup was tilted by faulting, producing the slanted rock layers seen today. Some segments of the Supergroup rose while others dropped. A long period of erosion stripped away the higher portions of this formation. The lower blocks, less touched by erosion, remained to make up the outcrops of the Supergroup seen irregularly in the canyon.

Great Unconformity

Between the Grand Canyon Supergroup and the next strata found in the canyon is a huge gap in the rock record. An estimated 12,000 feet of rock was deposited, only to be eroded before the next major deposition. Hundreds of millions of years of geological history are gone. Later sedimentation buried the Grand Canyon Supergroup, creating a gap or unconformity in the record. John Wesley Powell recognized the odd relationship between the older tilted rocks of the Supergroup and the younger flat-lying rock strata above, naming it the Great Unconformity.

The dipping layers of the Grand Canyon Supergroup lying under the horizontal layers of the Tapeats sandstone mark the point in the geological record known as the Great Unconformity. The unconformity marks a point where overlying strata were eroded away then re-covered with younger material, leaving a gap in the geological record.

Cambrian Rocks

Most of the exposed rock in the Grand Canyon, making up the cliffs and benches seen from the rims, was formed during the past 570 million to 250 million years. This period, the Paleozoic Era, represents the age of fishes. Among these rocks is the first substantial evidence of fossils. The Cambrian Period ended when a major catastrophe caused the exinction of 90 percent of the earth's animals.

During much of the Paleozoic Era, North America was united with Africa, Europe, and Antarctica into a supercontinent known as Pangaea.

About 570 million years ago, the western edge of Pangaea was inundated by successive seas, depositing layer after layer of sedimentary rock—limestone, sandstone, and siltstone. These layers have remained remarkably intact and make up most of the strata seen in the Grand Canyon.

Tonto Group

The Tonto Group is the oldest of the Cambrian Period sedimentary deposits in the canyon. It lies on top of the Great Unconformity of the Grand Canyon Supergroup. It consists of three ascending layers: Tapeats Sandstone, Bright Angel Shale, and Muav Limestone. The Tonto Platform—a prominent, nearly level bench that lies just above the Inner Gorge—is composed of Tonto Group rocks.

Each of these three strata represents deposits in an ocean. The Tapeats Sandstone was formed in the near-shore and beach areas where coarse, sandy cobbles were deposited. In the slightly deeper waters beyond the near-shore beach, finer mud sediments (that would later harden into the Bright Angel Shale) were laid down. Finally, in the deepest waters, a slimy calcium carbonate ooze settled out of the water to form the Muav Limestone.

These deposits were laid down as the margin, or edge, of the North American craton slowly subsided. The advancing edge of these deposits gradually moved eastward over millions of years so that the eastern portion of the deposits are younger than those in the west.

Fossils are rare in the Tonto Group, but invertebrates such as brachiopods, trilobites, and primitive mollusks and sponges are occasionally found.

The muds of the Bright Angel Shale easily erode into soft slopes, while the harder, better-cemented rocks of the Tapeats Sandstone and Muav Limestone form cliffs. Most of the surface of the Tonto Platform consists of the Tapeats Sandstone. Back from this flat rock surface lie the sloping cliffs of Bright Angel Shale, then comes the steep surface of the Muav Limestone.

There are outcrops of the Tonto Group elsewhere in the region. The Tapeats Sandstone makes up part of the Grand Wash Cliffs on the western edge of the Grand Canyon; it also crops out in central Arizona along the East Fork of the Verde River and Sierra Ancha Range.

The Tapeats Sandstone is named for outcrops of these strata found along Tapeats Creek in the western Grand Canyon. The Tapeats Sandstone consists of many thin beds or obvious layers of rock. It varies in thickness from 100 to 325 feet and forms the steep brown cliffs above the Vishnu Schist of the Granite Gorge.

Bright Angel Shale lies immediately above the Tapeats Sandstone and varies from 450 feet thick in the western Grand Canyon to 325 feet along Bright Angel Creek, for which the formation is named. Like the Tapeats Sandstone, the Bright Angel Shale crops out elsewhere, most notably in the Juniper Mountains north of Prescott, Arizona.

The Muav Limestone lies above the Bright Angel Shale. Like the other formations, its thickness varies. It is thinnest near the confluence of the Little Colorado River, where it is 136 feet thick, while at Grand Wash Cliffs, the layer is 827 feet thick.

Temple Butte Limestone

Another unconformity exists above the Tonto Group. Erosion stripped away all evidence of rocks that may have been formed during the Ordovician and Silurian periods. Eroded channels in the surface of the Muav Limestone suggests that water removed the overlying rocks. Resting on top of the Muav Limestone erosional platform is the Devonian-age Temple Butte Limestone. In some places, this limestone layer is 1,000 feet thick. The Temple Butte Limestone is not found everywhere in the canyon, but where it does occur, it often forms cliffs.

Redwall Limestone and Surprise Canyon Formation

The Redwall Limestone is a prominent part of the Grand Canyon sedimentary makeup. It forms vertical cliffs 500 to 800 feet high and is one of the biggest obstacles to trail construction. In most places where trails cut across the Redwall Limestone, they must be carved out of the rock. The stone itself is a dull gray, like most limestones, but has been stained red by iron oxide coming from overlying shales.

The Redwall Limestone settled in a shallow sea 330 million years ago. It is similar to other limestones found in southwestern Colorado, southeastern Nevada, and southeastern Arizona, likely representing widespread deposition in a shallow sea that once covered the region. This layer is full of fossils.

After deposition, the Redwall Limestone was uplifted and underwent karst erosion—a kind of erosion that occurs in limestone—common in

Near Grandview Point. The differences in how different rock strata erode are visible in this photo, which shows the contact point between the overlying Coconino sandstone (light tan) and red hermit shale below it.

humid limestone regions. Numerous caves and caverns were created during this period and later were filled with new sediment.

The Surprise Canyon Formation is not mentioned in older geological interpretations of the canyon. It was only recently discovered in remote parts of the western Grand Canyon and only occasionally appears as lens-shaped outcrops. It is named for Surprise Canyon, where a large outcrop is found. The formation developed in a shallow estuarine environment that covered the Redwall Limestone. The Surprise Canyon Formation fills V- or U-shaped drainage systems and collapsed karst caves notched into the erosional surface of the Redwall Limestone.

The Esplanade and Supai Group

The Esplanade is a name for one of the major cliff-forming sandstones in the upper sedimentary layers of the Grand Canyon rock strata known as the Supai Group. It was named by Clarence Dutton for the broad, open, level rock he found near Toroweap. All of the Supai Group rocks were formed in marine or coastal environments, including some fossilized coastal dune formations.

The Supai Group of red siltstones and sandstones were deposited in swampy, shallow water between 330 and 290 million years ago. Some cross bedding indicates the presence of coastal sand dunes. This was the beginning of the age of amphibians and their footprints are fossilized in some of these deposits. These rocks form prominent cliffs in the canyon.

Hermit Shale

Between 280 and 250 million years ago, the Hermit Shale was formed under similar conditions. The Hermit Shale contains evidence of flooding and retreat of seas, such as mud cracks, ripple marks, and footprints, all formed under shallow tidal conditions. The shale consists of softer rock than the Supai sandstones, so it erodes into a gentler slope. It is named for Hermit Basin along Hermit Canyon, where excellent outcrops are easily seen.

Coconino Sandstone

Toward the end of the Permian Period, a desert dominated the region, resulting in the formation of many steep cross-bedded sand dunes that later fossilized into the Coconino Sandstone. It forms yellowish tan cliffs. These rocks contain fossils of lizard tracks. This sandstone also crops out in Marble Canyon and the Mogollon Rim southeast of Flagstaff.

Toroweap Formation

The Toroweap Formation lies just below the Kaibab Limestone, which makes up the surface of the North and South rims. The Toroweap Formation is named for Toroweap Creek in the western end of the Grand

Cross bedding on Coconino sandstone on South Rim. Cross-bedded sandstones were deposited by winds in ancient sand dunes.

Canyon. It consists of sandstones and limestones whose hard, erosion-resistant rocks forms cliffs. Like the Coconino Sandstone, it crops out in other parts of the region, including the Mogollon Rim.

Kaibab Formation

The Kaibab Formation caps both rims of the canyon. It is named for the Kaibab Plateau on the North Rim. The Kaibab is primarily limestone up to 300 feet thick, and it forms cliffs. Limestone is easily carved by water and develops sinkholes and underground passages. Surface water readily finds its way underground, so the Kaibab Limestone is notoriously dry.

Beyond the Grand Canyon

The Kaibab Formation is the last Paleozoic Era rock visible in the canyon, but regional deposition of rock sediment did not end with this formation. The rocks of the Grand Canyon were covered by thousands of feet of sediment that has been eroded away. Red Butte south of Tusayan is a remnant of one these other younger rock formations that was not completely eroded. Younger rock strata are most easily observed in the plateau country to the north and east of the canyon. For example, the Kaibab Limestone is the lowest exposed rock layer in Zion National Park. All the other rock strata in Zion are younger than any rock group at the Grand Canyon.

The Mesozoic Era—or age of reptiles, including dinosaurs—began about 240 million years ago. It ended 65 million years ago with the extinction of the dinosaurs. During this period, sediment buried the Grand Canyon rocks. Toward the end of the Mesozoic, the North American plate collided with a number of other plates. The stresses threw up the Rocky Mountains and other ranges in the West. Faulting and uplifting also occurred around the Colorado Plateau, but most of the rocks stayed horizontal.

The Formation of the Canyon

Although the rocks exposed in the Grand Canyon are incredibly old, the canyon itself is young. Some believe it was carved during the past 2 million years, a speck of time compared with the 2-billion-year age of the rocks in the Inner Gorge. The entire canyon was sculpted during the last ice age, when humans were walking the planet. What also is interesting is the fact that the river cut across a mountain as well, the Kaibab Upwarp.

One theory suggests the Colorado River flowed from its headwaters in the Rockies through northeastern Arizona, perhaps southward along the present course of the Little Colorado River, to a large lake once found in eastern Arizona. It avoided the Kaibab Upwarp. Another stream to the west of the upwarp slowly carved its headwaters back into the Kaibab Upwarp. As a consequence, the stream broke through the watershed divide and "captured" the flow of the ancestral Colorado near the confluence of the Little Colorado.

A more recent theory suggests the Colorado always flowed across the Kaibab Upwarp but drained to the north. Once the Gulf of California opened, providing a low-elevation outlet, headwater erosion of what is now the lower Colorado captured the previously north-flowing ancestral Colorado.

Colorado River seen from Lipan Point on the South Rim. Though the Grand Canyon is deep, it is a relatively young geological feature, carved primarily during the past 2 million years.

Volcanic outcrop in Tuweep Valley. Recent volcanic flows cover portions of the western Grand Canyon.

Despite this uncertainty, there is little doubt that most of the canyon was formed during the last 2 million years. During this time, water flowing from ice age glaciers in the Rockies scoured away the overlying sedimentary rock. Since cutting into the very hard Vishnu Schist, the river's erosion has slowed considerably.

Volcanic Eruptions

Within the last million years, volcanoes near the canyon erupted. Lava poured over the landscape and down into the canyon more than 150 times. The source of these flows includes the Uinkaret Plateau, near the boundary between Lake Mead National Recreation Area and Grand Canyon National Park. Vulcans Throne near Toroweap Valley marks one of these recent flows. In some places, the lava poured over the rim of the canyon and fell thousands of feet, creating frozen lava falls.

Some lava in the western canyon even plugged the Colorado River, creating dams that were as much as 2,000 feet high. However, these dams

Colorado River seen at Tuweep (Toroweap) overlook. Lava flooding into the Colorado in this region created a number of natural dams that backed up the river, creating giant lakes.

were not like modern concrete constructions. Most filled a long stretch of the river channel; at least one occupied eighty-four miles of it. No fewer than twelve major lava dams have obstructed the river during the past million years. They backed up the river's flow sometimes as far as Utah, just beyond the slack water of Lake Powell. Typically, a lava dam fills the canyon in a matter of days, or at most a few weeks, an extremely rapid geological event. Geologists believe that most dams gave way long before the reservoirs behind them filled, causing tremendous floods that raced down the river channel.

VEGETATION

The Grand Canyon is a harsh environment for plants. Aridity and heat are the major factors, but the extremes in elevation mean that some places are too cold and snowy for growth. Most of the canyon, except for the highest elevations, lacks forests. Nevertheless, though the canyon was originally set aside as a geological wonder, there also is tremendous biological diversity, in part due to the 8,000-foot difference in elevation between the desert along the river corridor and the subalpine forest on the Kaibab Plateau. More than 1,500 plant species live in the park.

The inner canyon can be characterized as arid and hot (up to 120 degrees along the Colorado River). Extremes are the norm, with hot days followed by chilly nights. Plants of the canyon have adapted to allow them to thrive under such conditions. Plants from three out of four of North America's major deserts (the Mojave, Sonoran, and Great Basin) are found here.

The lowest, hottest parts of the canyon are dominated by plants of the Mojave Desert. The Colorado River forms a low-elevation environment where plants from this ecosystem penetrate upstream. Also mixing in the canyon are plants like ocotillo, more typical of the Sonoran Desert farther south, and of cold-desert species like sagebrush that dominate so much of the Great Basin in Nevada, southern Idaho, and eastern Oregon.

At the other extreme, the forests on the Kaibab Plateau have reminders of locations much farther north. Here are stands of subalpine fir, a species common in the northern Rockies and Canada, along with Douglas fir, white fir, Engelmann spruce, blue spruce, and aspen. All of these trees more or less dominate higher elevations in the Rockies, and in essence, the Kaibab Plateau represents the southern extension of this great mountain chain.

Most of the plant communities are divided by elevation. All things being equal, temperatures and moisture change from the lowest elevations to the highest. As you ascend a mountain (or, in this case, the canyon), the average temperature drops and precipitation increases.

C. Hart Merriam of the U.S. Biological Survey first noted this relationship while exploring the Grand Canyon region in 1889. He observed that the changes in plant communities encountered by climbing a mountain in Arizona were like traveling thousands of miles north. Plants growing near the summit of the San Francisco Peaks by Flagstaff or the Kaibab Plateau on the north side of the Grand Canyon had more in common with those in Canada than they did with the surrounding lowland species. These observations gave rise to Merriam's famous "Life Zone" concept, developed to explain his observations of plant and animal distribution. The concept is now considered too crude to account for all the variables that affect species distribution, but it still has some merit.

Another influence on plant distribution is topography. Cold air drains down valleys and sinks off of ridges. Thus you'll find hardy species fingering down valleys into the warmer desert areas and warmth-loving species climbing ridges to cooler elevation zones.

Aspen fringes a meadow at Crane Lake on the Kaibab Plateau, Kaibab National Forest.

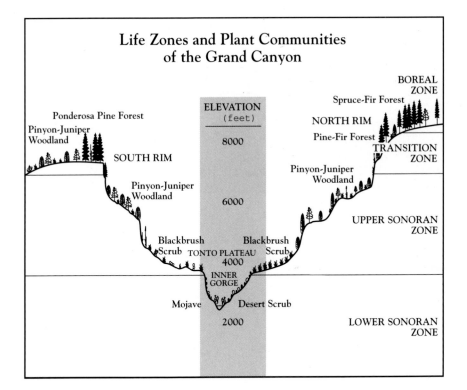

Life Zones and Plant Communities of the Grand Canyon

Within the Grand Canyon there is even a special influence: warm updrafts near the canyon rim. These blasts moderate conditions on the North Rim in particular, allowing some species to live at higher elevations than they might otherwise find suitable.

Plants in the Desert

Plants in arid regions have three ways of dealing with the limitations of water.

1. Plants that conserve water and endure aridity. Many desert plants do not need much water and often can store it for long periods. Cacti are a good example of this plant group. A barrel cactus has an extensive root system that gathers water from a wide area and stores it within its cells like a giant sponge.

Other plants have modified their structure to reduce water loss. Since leaves lose water, many desert plants have small or pinnate leaves like those found on mesquite, sagebrush, antelope brush, and mountain

Prickly pear cactus. Cactus can store water and survive for years, if necessary, without any rainfall.

mahogany. In addition, many of these leaves have waxy or thick coatings that reduce water loss, as in manzanita. Another common adaptation designed to reduce water loss is hairy leaves. Fine hairs mitigate the effects of wind, slowing evaporative water loss.

Some plants take leaf modifications to the extreme and drop their leaves altogether. The coachwhip-like ocotillo, for example, sprouts leaves after rainy periods but drops them in drought. The waxy green leaves of creosote bush display a similar adaptation. Sagebrush has larger leaves that it sprouts in spring, when soil moisture is highest, and smaller leaves it retains during drought. Cacti have taken this to the extreme, dispensing with leaves or having only temporary, rudimentary ones. To photosynthesize, most cacti have green stalks that act in the same manner as leaves, producing food for the plant.

2. Plants that avoid drought. Some plants avoid drought by growing only when water is available. Grasses are a good example of this adaptation. Many green up and grow during the season when warmth and moisture are suitable, then drop their seeds and go dormant once water becomes scarce or temperatures reach extremes. Many annual and perennial flowers also fit into this category, blooming in the spring or early summer when soil moisture is highest.

Seeds are a particularly effective means of avoiding drought. Many desert plants have seeds that can remain dormant in the soil for years, sprouting only when moisture is sufficient. To ensure sprouting only at such times, some seeds even have special water-soluble chemical coatings that inhibit germination until they have been washed away by rain.

3. Plants that do not experience aridity. There are some plants, primarily those along the Colorado River or its tributaries or near springs, that do not experience drought. They have lots of water and consume it freely. Most riparian zone plants fit into this category. Cottonwoods and maidenhair fern grow only where plenty of water is available. Some, like the cottonwood, have large leaves that lose enormous amounts of water into the atmosphere.

There are several notable characteristics of drought-resistant plants. Many take on a rounded, cluttered shape. From sagebrush to juniper, this general growth form helps to reduce water losses by providing shade to leaves inside the clump.

Many desert plants also have extensive root systems that allow them to tap soil moisture over a wide region or at great depth. Grasses, for example, are like inverted trees, with most of their mass in their root systems. Often a grass plant that is only a foot high above ground may have a root mat extending down into the soil three to four feet. Mesquite trees have deep taproots; one in southern Arizona was found to have a root reaching down 175 feet!

Mormon tea has many special adaptations for survival in the desert. It has a rounded, densely packed cluster of "leaves" that reduces water loss.

Plants in the Snow Belt

Plants in the higher Kaibab Plateau often have opposite problems from desert species. Cold and snow are dominant. Nearly all of the higher-elevation plants are perennial. Many of the trees found high on the Kaibab Plateau have adapted to deep snow. The narrow crown of sub-alpine fir helps the tree to shed snow without breaking its branches. Its boughs are flexible, easily bending under heavy snow.

Aspen and other broad-leaved deciduous trees like Gambel's oak lose their leaves in winter; otherwise, they would capture too much snow and branches likely would snap.

Given the deep snows and short growing season on the plateau, conifers dominate over deciduous trees. The evergreen conifers can photosynthesize throughout the year. As long as the air temperature rises above freezing, photosynthesis is possible, even if roots and lower branches are under snow. This gives conifers an advantage over all but the fastest-growing deciduous species.

Fire Ecology

Before the white man came to the Southwest, wildfires periodically burned vast areas of the region. The ponderosa pine forests on both rims experienced wildfires on an average of every three to fifteen years. The frequency and intensity of blazes, however, varied considerably, depending upon the amount of fuel (known as fuel loading), weather conditions, age and species of plants, and other factors. As a rule, very arid areas rarely burned due to the bare soil and scarcity of plants, and forests such as those growing above 8,500 feet on the Kaibab Plateau experienced infrequent, though intense, blazes because of the long snow season and the high moisture content of soil and vegetation.

Most fires are started by lightning in summer. Indians also ignited blazes to clear brush or enhance wildlife habitat; on occasion, they simply let a campfire get out of control, as happens today. Wildfires were such a continual and important ecological influence that many species evolved to cope with them. Wildfire is now recognized as a critical part of healthy plant communities, including grassland, shrubland, and forest.

Wildfire helps these ecosystems by recycling nutrients. This is particularly true in many western ecosystems, where the cold and aridity inhibit biological decomposition. In addition, fires prepare seed beds; provide a mosaic of age classes and vegetative types; cleanse forests and other plant communities of fungi, insects, and other pathogens; and reduce fire hazards.

Yet we still have no positive way of describing this important process. We continue to be biased against blazes. How often do we hear of how a wildfire "destroyed" so many acres of forest or how a "disastrous" fire charred such and such a mountainside? Certainly if a house or barn were destroyed, we might consider it a loss, but in terms of the forest, wildfires are as normal and necessary as winter snows for replenishing western watersheds. Although it may sound contrived, a more accurate description of the aftermath of a blaze would be to suggest that the fire created wildlife habitat or rejuvenated the forest. It is not fires but the absence of fires, including big ones, that poses the gravest threat to most western landscapes.

Until recently, it was common to fight all fires, no matter the origin. Firefighting started around the turn of the century, and as a consequence, many plant communities throughout the West have changed. When Clarence Dutton rode across the Kaibab Plateau in 1881, he described the pine forests as "open and park-like." Today, many of these forests look like thickets, with dense understories of white fir. What these forests need is a good blaze, an insect outbreak, or some other form of natural destruction to thin some trees and reset the balance.

Forests have also encroached upon the meadows that once laced the uplands. However, in contrast to the effects of firefighting on the pine and meadow communities, the spruce forests appear to have changed little. Even in Dutton's time, they were described as clustering "so thickly together that a passage through them is extremely difficult and sometimes impossible."

Furthermore, firefighting has been successful for only four or five decades, not nearly long enough to completely disrupt forest processes. The first successful firefighting programs in the Grand Canyon began in the 1930s, with the construction of lookout towers, roads to speed access for firefighters, and the seasonal hiring of a trained firefighting force. By the 1970s, research on the importance of fire in forest ecosystems led to a change in policy. The park adopted a plan that defined the conditions under which fires could resume a more natural role in the park. Today, naturally caused fires are permitted to burn under prescribed conditions. The factors include the availability of firefighting equipment and personnel, the danger to buildings and people, and effects upon air quality. Under ideal conditions, fires are permitted to run their course.

Most people assume that it is the presence of fuel, particularly dead trees, that determines whether a fire burns, but the most important influence is weather. In most years, regardless of fuel, wildfires cannot burn. Indeed, most fires started by lightning burn themselves out without consuming even an acre. Without the proper weather conditions, fires do not burn. Nearly all large fires result from extreme weather conditions, including extensive drought, high temperatures, and wind. Wind, in

In the absence of fire, young ponderosa pines invade meadows. Years of fire suppression have led to a significant change in the forest appearance, with a higher density of small trees replacing the more typical open forest of large trees that existed in presuppression days.

particular, appears to be a critical element. The majority of acres burned in any fire year occurs on a few days when a fire "runs" before a wind. Despite images in *Bambi* of wildlife fleeing before a wall of flames, most fires sputter and crawl rather than race their way through a forest.

In addition, under extreme conditions, it is green trees, not dead ones, that pose the greatest fire hazard. Most pines, firs, and spruces contain highly flammable resins. Under extreme drought, trees dry out sufficiently to carry a flame and the resins actually make the trees more combustible, as if they were doused in gasoline.

Most wildfires create a "mosaic" of burned and unburned tree stands.

A gust of wind may push a blaze through one section of forest while skirting another stand. One slope may be too wet to burn while another is dry enough to carry a blaze. A forest with a dense understory of flammable young trees may carry the blaze into the crown of the forest in some areas while passing by another section that lacks an understory. The point

Gambel oak. This tree will sprout from its roots after a fire.

Young ponderosa pines killed by fire, Kaibab Plateau. Such fires thin the forest, promoting the growth of the remaining trees.

is that even under similar weather conditions, wildfires do not destroy entire forests.

The Grand Canyon receives much of its precipitation as snow. As it melts, deadwood and other fuels are saturated. There is a long delay that extends into summer when most fuels are simply too wet to burn. In normal precipitation years, the South Rim's vegetation and fuels do not dry sufficiently to carry a blaze until mid-July, and the higher North Rim may not reach that stage until August. By September, with the shorter days, cool nights, higher humidity, and occasional snowstorms, the trends begin to reverse. Thus, in most years, there is actually little opportunity for forest fires. July and August are the primary months for wildfires.

As mentioned earlier, most fires burn themselves out quickly simply

Fire scar on ponderosa pine. Larger trees usually survive the common fires in ponderosa pine forests.

from a lack of fuel or improper weather conditions. From 1931 to 1980 (when fire suppression was the norm), only 51 fires out of 1,537 were larger than 10 acres or more. Only 8 of these were larger than 300 acres. The largest blaze in recent years, the Saddle Mountain Fire, was on the Kaibab Plateau and burned 11,000 acres of forest inside the park and adjacent U.S. Forest Service lands.

These figures point out that small, frequent fires are important but may not control forest ecosystems. Larger, less frequent burns actually shape forest composition, age, and structure. Indeed, just as an occasional harsh winter may significantly reduce a deer herd with no long-term effect upon the deer population, the occasional large fire doesn't really destroy a forest. And, contrary to common practice, we should encourage large, intense fires as much as smaller burns. Just as a 100-year flood affects the hydrology of a stream channel differently than the average annual flood, the occasional large fire may be necessary for forest ecosystems to work properly.

Fire and Forest Communities

Perhaps the most recognized role of wildfires has been among the ponderosa pine forests of the West. In Grand Canyon National Park, ponderosa occupies 21,000 acres or about 1.7 percent of the park, mostly on the Kaibab Plateau. Nevertheless, ponderosa is a major component on forest service lands just outside the park.

Fire history research in and around the Grand Canyon has shown that before modern firefighting, fires burned through southwestern ponderosa forests every three to fifteen years. This is likely because these forests are wet enough to be greener than adjacent desert areas but still are open enough to dry out quickly in summer.

Although fires were frequent, do not envision walls of flames. Most of these fires were of a low intensity, creeping through the forest primarily on grasses and dried needles on the ground. They occasionally burned up thickets of young pines but seldom seriously harmed mature trees.

Ponderosa has numerous adaptations that allow it to survive and even thrive under these periodic low-intensity blazes. Perhaps the most obvious are its thick, scaly bark and self-pruning bole. The bark insulates the living tissue from all but the most intense heat. In addition, as the tree grows older, it sheds its lower branches, creating a branchless bole that prevents flames from jumping into the tree crown. The buds of the growing branches also are heat resistant.

Within the wetter, higher spruce-fir forest that dominates the Kaibab Plateau, wildfires were less frequent but more intense. These forests cloak 59,000 acres (4.8 percent) of the park, almost exclusively on the North Rim.

Not only does snow linger at these elevations, but overall conditions are cooler because of the lower average temperatures as well as the shade created by the forest's dense canopies. These woodlands take longer to dry out. Most larger fires here are of a "stand-replacement" nature; they kill many of the older trees. The interval between fires may be several hundred years or more. Blue spruce, Engelmann spruce, and subalpine fir have little resistance to fires, with thin bark and limited self-pruning. In addition, the needles and wood contain resins. Two other species, Douglas and white fir, are susceptible to fire when young, having thin bark and lower branches. Unlike the other three, as these species mature, their bark thickens and lower branches self-prune, providing many of the advantages of ponderosa.

Just below the ponderosa zone lies the pinyon-juniper forest, which makes up 7.7 percent of the Grand Canyon's woodlands. Lying between 4,000 and 7,000 feet, this type is found in the drier parts of the park. Although the dry conditions favor fires, the limited moisture reduces plant growth, and, in turn, fuel. An abundance of rocks and bare dirt also inhibits blazes.

As a rule, pinyon pine and juniper are not particularly fire resistant. When young, they have thin bark and low branches. As they mature, their bark thickens and they lose some of their lower branches. Few fires in this habitat spread far. Nevertheless, given the long-lived nature of these species, particularly juniper (which may survive 1,000 years or more), fire probably helps determine where pinyon and juniper grow. Most older junipers and pinyons have been restricted to rocky areas where fire is limited by available fuels.

In the desert shrub community found between 3,000 and 6,000 feet, natural fire intervals are less frequent than among the ponderosa forests but more frequent than in the high spruce-fir areas. Aridity keeps plant productivity low, limiting fuel. Nevertheless, under certain conditions, shrub areas will burn, particularly if there is a lot of grass, which is a "flashy" fuel. Some species, like rabbitbrush and four-wing saltbush, are root sprouters; almost immediately after a fire, new shoots develop from the unburned underground roots. Other species, like some sagebrushes and blackbrush, do not sprout from roots and rely upon reseeding from unburned plants. Sagebrush fires often produce grasslands in which sagebrush gradually returns over thirty to fifty years.

Although firefighting is often cited as changing forest structure and age, livestock grazing is only beginning to be appreciated in this regard. The cropping of fine fuels like grass combined with soil compaction (which reduces water absorption) are thought to change natural plant communities. Some scientists believe the spread of juniper savannas, the reduction of fire frequency among ponderosa forests, and the spread of sagebrush can be ascribed to grazing.

Where fires are frequent, as among ponderosa, saplings are killed, leaving behind an open forest dominated by mature trees. Fire suppression and perhaps grazing have reduced this natural thinning, allowing flammable young thickets of pine and white fir to grow. Fuels also have accumulated. The result in some instances has been hotter, more intense fires.

Nevertheless, its important to note that large, intense fires have always occurred. Though frequent, low-intensity fires are the norm, they represent averages, not absolutes. There have always been stands of timber that, for whatever reasons, were skipped repeatedly by fires. In addition, during extreme drought, even open parklike forests can burn intensely if flames reach the crowns, which occurs with high winds.

Conversely, despite the average fire frequency of three to fifteen years in many ponderosa forests historically, the fifty years or so of fire suppression in the park probably have not radically altered forests beyond natural conditions. If viewed over the past 1,000 years or more, there have been extensive periods in which wet, cool weather inhibited fires for decades, sometimes centuries, creating conditions not unlike those of today. With drier conditions, large fires burned across the landscape, setting back succession to the more recent historic frequency.

We need a new appreciation, tolerance, and respect for the ecological importance of fire. As with predators, fires have an essential role in maintaining the health of the forest ecosystem. To paraphrase Aldo Leopold, who once admonished game managers to protect predators because they helped to maintain the vigor of the deer herd, I suggest that if a forest ecosystem could speak, it would say it lives in mortal fear not of fire but of fire suppression. Just as we should protect and reintroduce predators wherever possible, we should encourage the tolerance of wildfires.

Major Plant Communities and Distribution

Riparian Communities

Along the Colorado River and its tributaries lies a narrow greenbelt of water-dependent vegetation known as the riparian community. Such plants are often the only wooded vegetation found below 5,000 feet and are confined to waterways, seeps, and springs. Common species include Fremont cottonwood, salt cedar or tamarisk, willows, seep-willow, and honey mesquite.

Associated species, not all strictly riparian but found in or adjacent to riparian areas, include catclaw acacia, Apache plume, monkeyflower, canyon grape, redbud, Arizona alder, box elder, and desert holly.

Lower Sonoran Zone

Below 2,000 feet lies the driest and hottest part of the Grand Canyon, dominated by desert shrubs such as creosote bush, white bursage, ocotillo, brittlebush, and cacti like barrel and cholla. At the very western edge of the canyon are pockets of Joshua tree and desert grasslands.

Other associated species include rayless encelia, catclaw acacia, hedgehog cactus, prickly pear cactus, beavertail cactus, desert mallow, and jimmy weed.

Upper Sonoran Zone

The Upper Sonoran Zone lies between 2,000 and 7,000 feet. There are five major plant communities in this zone: blackbrush, sagebrush, grasslands, mountain shrub, and pinyon-juniper woodland. Each has its own characteristic vegetation.

BLACKBRUSH

This desert shrub community dominates the lower, drier habitat between 3,500 and 5,000 feet on flat to rolling terrain such as the Tonto and Sanup plateaus. Plants include blackbrush, mountain joint fir, banana yucca, and snakeweed.

SAGEBRUSH

Above the blackbrush communities at cooler elevations up to 7,000 feet, including on the rims, grows the gray-green shrub sagebrush. Sagebrush forms a more or less evenly spaced ground cover over extensive areas on the Kanab Plateau, the west side of the Kaibab Plateau, and parts of the South Rim. It also grows among trees within the pinyon-juniper woodlands.

Associated species include snakeweed, prickly pear cactus, rabbitbrush, western wheatgrass, cliffrose, and blue grama.

GRASSLANDS

Grasslands are restricted within the Upper Sonoran to the top of the Grand Wash Cliffs and Toroweap Valley. Species on top of the Grand Wash Cliffs at 4,700 to 5,200 feet include black grama, red brome, and associated shrubs including winter fat and four-wing saltbush.

Native bunchgrass in the Tuweep (Toroweap) Valley in the western Grand Canyon.

In the slightly lower Toroweap Valley, which has been heavily over-grazed, common plants include grasses like big galleta, Indian ricegrass, and the exotic cheatgrass. Associated shrubs include winterfat, four-wing saltbush, and snakeweed.

MOUNTAIN SHRUB

Growing just below the rims on talus slopes and rocky ledges between 4,000 and 7,000 feet is the mountain shrub community. Evergreen chaparral species include manzanita, silktassel, and scrub oak. Deciduous species include serviceberry, wavyleaf oak, and New Mexican locust.

Associated species include snowberry, fendlerbush, banana yucca, rabbitbrush, barberry, cliffrose, mountain mahogany, and serviceberry.

PINYON-JUNIPER WOODLAND

At the highest parts of the Upper Sonoran Zone (up to 7,000 feet) grow open woodlands of pinyon-juniper. Shrubby trees include Utah juniper, pinon pine, and sometimes the deciduous Gambel oak. Often, sagebrush and rabbitbrush are found in the understory.

Other species in pinyon-juniper woodlands include Utah serviceberry, cliffrose, paintbrush, Apache plume, Utah agave, prickly pear cactus, banana yucca, buckwheat, mountain joint fir, and blue grama.

Sagebrush.

Pinyon pine cone and needles. The shrubby growing pinyon pine possesses cones that contain large seeds. These seeds, or pinyon "nuts," were an important food source for Native Americans, as well as many animal species.

Transition Zone

The transition zone lies between 6,500 and 7,400 feet. This is where grasslands and shrublands give way to full-fledged forests. The dominant tree of the transition zone is ponderosa pine. Extensive open stands of ponderosa grow on higher portions of the South Rim, such as near Grand Canyon Village, as well as on the Kaibab Plateau, the Mount Trumbull area, and higher parts of the Hualapai Reservation and Shivwits Plateau. Other species growing among the pine include Gambel's oak and white fir. White fir is particularly common among the pine on the North Rim.

Associated species include wild rose, snowberry, lupine, little-leaf mountain mahogany, redroot eriogonum , blue grama, beard tongue, skunkbush, western wheatgrass, phlox, and fernbush.

Canadian Zone

This zone occurs only north of the Colorado River, primarily on the Kaibab Plateau above 8,000 feet. There are two major types of plant communities: fir-aspen-mixed coniferous forest and mountain grasslands.

White barked aspen, a common tree on the North Rim.

FIR-ASPEN-MIXED CONIFEROUS FOREST

This type is dominated by Douglas fir, white fir, and quaking aspen. Pockets of such forest can be found in shady areas on north-facing cliffs just below the South Rim.

Understory species include Utah serviceberry, ocean spray, wormwood, agave, gooseberry, wild rose, creeping mahonia, and sticky gooseberry.

MOUNTAIN GRASSLANDS

Mountain grasslands or meadows tend to occupy depressions and relatively flat areas on the Kaibab Plateau. They are found between 7,800 feet and 9,100 feet in the Canadian and Hudsonian zones, sometimes collectively called the Boreal Zone. Mountain grasslands are dominated by perennial grasses like Letterman needlegrass, mountain muhly, bearded wheatgrass, timothy, orchard grass, tufted hairgrass, brome, and Kentucky bluegrass.

Wildflowers are abundant, including giant hyssop, sandwort, bellflower, paintbrush, fireweed, running fleabane, red-root buckwheat, gentian, flax, tarweed, bluebells, beard tongue or penstemon, buttercup, sheep sorrel, goldenrod, and goldeneye.

Blue flax grows on both rims and in the canyon.

Hudsonian Zone

SPRUCE-FIR FOREST

This type is at the highest elevations of the Kaibab Plateau, usually above 8,800 feet. Dominant trees include Engelmann spruce, white fir, subalpine fir, and aspen. Blue spruce is often found in wetter sites in depressions.

Other species associated with these forests include creeping mahonia, snowberry, deer vetch, bracken fern, cranesbill, gooseberry, and wild rose.

Cyptogramic crust covers soil. These crusts help to reduce erosion and enrich soils by adding nitrogen. Such crusts are fragile and are easily destroyed by livestock, off-road vehicle use, and even careless hikers who travel off-trail.

Species Accounts

Rather than attempt to describe every plant found in the Grand Canyon, I'll review the more obvious and dominant species, primarily trees and common shrubs. Those interested in more information can consult an excellent monograph, *Annotated Checklist of Vascular Plants of Grand Canyon National Park,* by Barbara Phillips, Arthur Phillips, and Marilyn Schmidt Bernzott.

Trees

PONDEROSA PINE
(Pinus ponderosa)

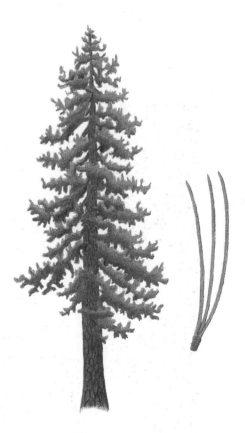

Description. Reddish orange to yellowish, scaly bark. Tall, up to 100 feet, straight, often branchless lower bole. Has longish needles (five to ten inches) in groups of three. Roundish cones are three to six inches long and prickly. Some people say the bark smells something like vanilla.

Distribution. Most common between 6,000 and 8,000 feet. On the South Rim, typically restricted to areas above 7,200 feet. Grandview Point is a good place to see mature ponderosa pine forest on the South Rim. Pockets of ponderosa, however, follow cool-air drainage to slightly lower elevations. Thus scattered pockets are seen around Grand Canyon Village and at shady spots below the rim. Ponderosa also forms extensive open woodlands on the Kaibab Plateau of the North Rim in the transition between open grasslands and shrublands and in higher, moister forests usually dominated by spruce and fir.

Remarks. Ponderosa can live as long as 600 years. They have an extensive root system that may reach as much as 100 feet below the bole. Given the droughty conditions often prevailing in its preferred habitat, a large root network is an adaptation to arid conditions. Ponderosa usually grows in rather park-like stands. This aspect is maintained by

Red-barked trunk of ponderosa pine on North Rim. The self-pruning of lower branches and the thick bark of mature trees helps older ponderosa pines survive fires.

periodic fires that kill younger trees but spare the mature ones. In the Grand Canyon region before modern firefighting, ponderosa forests burned on an average of every three to fifteen years. (For more on fire ecology and adaptations of ponderosa pine and other species, read the fire ecology section of the chapter on vegetation.) Fire suppression has left many pine stands densely stocked.

DOUGLAS FIR
(Pseudotsuga menziesii)

Description. Height to 100 feet. Needles are 1 to 1.5 inches and flat. Stems are covered with needles all around, giving a bottle-brush appearance. Cones are two to three inches with a distinctive three-pronged bract (said to look a like the hind legs of a mouse with a tail) protruding from scales. Cones hang down from branches. Bark is grayish to reddish brown, corky, and rough in older trees, and smooth gray in young ones.

Distribution. Typically found between 6,500 and 9,150 feet. A co-dominant at higher elevations on the North Rim and on north-facing slopes and alcoves of Toroweap Formation below South Rim.

Remarks. The Douglas fir sometimes attains an age of 1,000 years. Named for early botanist David Douglas. It is adapted to periodic fire, having thick bark and self-pruning lower branches. One of the major timber species in the West; there are several subspecies. The Rocky Mountain Douglas fir can tolerate drier conditions but does not grow as large as its Pacific Northwest cousin.

WHITE FIR
(Abies concolor)

Description. Height to 100 feet. Smooth, whitish bark. Needles one to three inches, flat with narrow white grooves on bottom side, giving a frosted appearance. Needles curve up from side of branch. Cone 5.5 inches long and greenish yellow; sits erect on branch. Cones seldom found intact on the ground, since like all firs, the cones disintegrate on branch.

Distribution. Found between 7,000 and 9,000 feet. Common on North Rim, often mixed with ponderosa. On South Rim, found only on north-facing slopes below rim by Grandview and Yaki points.

White fir, a shade-tolerant species, is invading the understory of this aspen grove. In the absence of fire, the fir will eventually shade out the aspen.

White fir in the understory of ponderosa pine, Kaibab Plateau. Over time, the shade-tolerant white fir will eventually grow up and replace the sun-loving pine at some sites.

Remarks. This tree is native to central and southern Rockies as well as Sierra Nevada and Cascades. It reaches its southern limits in northern Arizona. Susceptible to fire and easily killed. With fire suppression has greatly spread and increased in density, and has invaded the understory of mature ponderosa pine on the North Rim.

SUBALPINE FIR
(Abies lasiocarpa)

Description. Height to ninety feet. Narrow, pointed profile, with branches reaching nearly to the ground and bent downward to shed snow. Gray bark is usually quite smooth, with horizonal resin blisters, though the lower bole of older trees may become fissured. Flat needles up to one inch long and dark bluish green. Needles crowd upward pointing from twig. Cones purple and usually less than two inches long. Like all fir cones, they disintegrate on the tree.
Distribution. Found between 8,500 and 9,150 feet among the higher elevations of the Kaibab Plateau on North Rim.
Remarks. This tree has no protection against fire. Indeed, its volatile oils burn almost like gasoline. Lower branches can reach the ground, often forming a "ladder" on which flames can reach the crown of forest.

ENGELMANN SPRUCE
(Picea engelmannii)

Description. Height to 80 to 100 feet. Regular tiers of branches. Bark is thin with reddish gray scales. Needles are one inch long and four-sided, not flattened. They round in your fingers. Pointed, so can be prickly. Cones hang down from branches and are one to two inches long, light brown, with scales that have wavy edges.
Distribution. Grows between 8,400 and 9,150 feet, on North Rim only.
Remarks. This tree lives up to 450 years. In other parts of the West, often grows near timberline, where it takes on a stunted, twisted form.

Engelmann spruce growing here on the edge of a meadow are found at higher elevations on the North Rim. Spruce needles are prickly to the touch.

BLUE SPRUCE
(Picea pungens)

Description. Height to eighty feet. Narrow, conical shape. Needles are four-sided and prickly to touch. Brown bark. Trees vary in "blueness," but often do have a bluish cast. Cones are four inches long and brown with wavy-edged scales.
Distribution. North Rim only. Fairly rare. Spotty distribution on Kaibab Plateau. Seldom grows in large stands. Typical along watercourses and the edges of wet meadows.
Remarks. May approach 800 years of age.

PINYON PINE
(Pinus edulis)

Description. Small, seldom more than thirty feet. Often many-trunked and shrubby looking. Reddish bark. Needles one to two inches in groups of two. Cones are egg-shaped and brown, about two inches long. Scales lack prickles.

Distribution. Found between 4,000 and 7,000 feet. Dominant in woodlands on South Rim, including inner canyon down to redwall formation. Found on North Rim as well, but less frequently. Can be seen at Cape Royal and Tiyo Point.

Remarks. This tree often grows with Utah juniper to form the pinyon-juniper woodland. Pinyon produces a large seed that is favored by birds and mammals. Humans also collect the seeds as pine nuts. The cones take three years to mature and produce only twenty to thirty seeds per cone. Good crops occur only once every five to seven years. Pinyons can live for 400 years. A similar species, single-leaf pinyon (Pinus monophylla), is sometimes encountered in a few locations on the north side of the river.

UTAH JUNIPER
(Juniperus osteosperma)

Description. Small, usually less than twenty feet tall, often with many-stemmed trunks. Gray, shredded bark. Yellowish green, with overlapping scaly leaves. Cones are less than a quarter inch wide and bluish, about the size of a small marble. The berry turns reddish brown with age.

Distribution. Between 4,000 and 7,000 feet. Common in the pinyon-juniper woodland. Found on both rims, but more common on South. Also found inside canyon from rim to top of redwall formation.

Remarks. Both juniper and pinyon produce chemical compounds that discourage herbivores and the growth of

Utah juniper.

plants that might compete for water—one reason the ground beneath these trees often has little vegetation.

The Utah juniper is one of four junipers found in the canyon; the others are less common. One is dwarf juniper (*Juniperus communis*), a small shrub. The others reach small tree size; they are one-seed juniper (*Juniperus monosperma*) and Rocky Mountain juniper (*Juniperus scopulorum*). The Utah juniper almost always has a definite trunk, while one-seed juniper is more shrubby, with multiple stems rising from ground.

ASPEN
(*Populus tremuloides*)

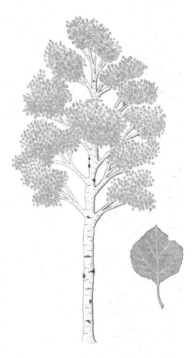

Description. Usually not more than forty feet tall. White bark with straight boles. Leaves are roundish, about one inch in diameter, with flattened stem. Tree self-prunes lower branches. Leaf color is beautiful lime green in spring, apple green in summer, and golden, or sometimes reddish, in autumn.

Distribution. Grows from 7,000 to 9,000 feet. One of the most widely distributed trees in North America. Within Grand Canyon National Park, most abundant on North Rim Kaibab Plateau, but also found in a few higher areas of South Rim.

Remarks. Grows in genetically identical clones. Often an entire patch of trees on a hillside will change color simultaneously, often outlining the extent of the individual clone. Seldom established from seeds; roots of existing trees put up "suckers" or stems that grow into mature trees. Aspens are favored by natural disturbances like fire; their trunks are important for bird nesting.

The thin-barked aspen dies easily in fires, but sprouts new boles from its roots.

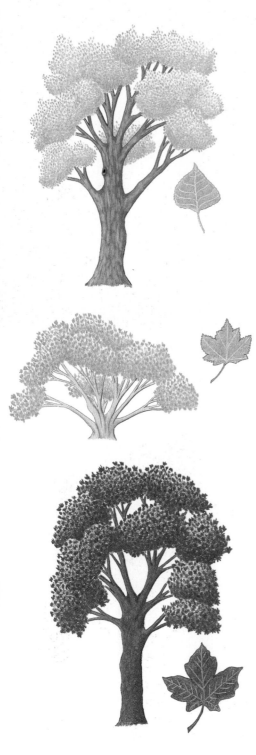

FREMONT COTTONWOOD
(*Populus fremontii*)

Description. Height from 60 to 100 feet. Has spreading crown with drooping branches. Great shade tree. Leaves are large, green, triangular. Bark is light gray and deeply furrowed on older trees.
Distribution. A riparian species, always associated with water. Found in the Colorado River corridor and many tributaries like Havasu and Bright Angel, and at Indian Gardens.
Remarks. Named for explorer John C. Fremont. An important wildlife tree in the riparian zone, providing nesting and roosting habitat for dozens of species, including hawks, eagles, bats, great blue herons, and many songbirds.

ROCKY MOUNTAIN MAPLE
(*Acer glabrum*)

Description. Shrubby tree, seldom more than fifteen feet tall. Opposite leaves, strongly toothed with three to five lobes. Turns golden in autumn. Bark is smooth and light gray.
Distribution. Found on North and South rims on moist, rich soils in openings among coniferous forests.
Remarks. Exceptional deer and elk food.

BIGTOOTH MAPLE
(*Acer saccharum* var. *grandidentatum*)

Description. Shrubby tree to thirty feet. Leaves to four inches, with blunt teeth and three major lobes. Gray, thin bark.
Distribution. Elevation from 6,500 to 8,200 feet. Often mixed among coniferous forest with moist soils, primarily below North Rim.
Remarks. Turns scarlet in autumn, adding much to fall colors on the North Rim.

Bigtooth maple, common on the North Rim, is related to the sugar maple of the eastern United States. Its foliage turns bright crimson in the autumn, adding much to the color found on the North Rim.

GAMBEL OAK
(Quercus gambelii)

Description. Usually less than thirty feet. Leafless during the winter. In summer, the two- to six-inch leaves are dark, green, and shiny with deep, rounded lobes with smooth edges. Rough, scaly, grayish bark. Often many trunked, thicket-like. Red leaves in autumn.

Distribution. Both rims of canyon and in shady areas just below rim. Usually associated with ponderosa.

Remarks. Leaves are shiny due to a waxy substance designed to reduce water loss. Can sprout from roots, especially if the main crown is destroyed by fire or heavy animal browsing. Many oak stands are actually genetically identical clones descended from one individual.

Gambel oak on the North Rim. Acorns from oaks are an important food source for wildlife including deer, bears, and wild turkeys.

SALTCEDAR
(Tamarix ramosissima)

Description. Short tree to twenty feet. Leaves are scalelike and branches appear feathery. In spring, small, pink flowers in terminal spikes give the impression of cotton candy. Deciduous.

Distribution. Riparian species, primarily along Colorado River corridor.

Remarks. This is an introduced tree, sometimes called tamarisk, that has spread throughout riparian areas in the Southwest. It has become important in the riparian zone since Glen Canyon Dam changed the river flow.

Shrubs

SKUNK BUSH
(Rhus trilobata)

Description. Height to seven feet. Leaves three-lobed leaflets each one inch long, with scalloped shallow lobes. Tiny flowers are yellowish and bloom in spike-like clusters that come out before leaves. Fruit is red berry.
Distribution. Brushy, rocky areas 3,500 to 7,000 feet on South Rim, but upper elevations in canyon. Also near Toroweap Valley.
Remarks. Has foul odor. Berries are sometimes used to make a lemonade-tasting beverage. In autumn, the leaves turn bright red, adding much to the colors of the canyon.

SERVICEBERRY
(Amelanchier utahensis)

Description. Many-trunked stems to fifteen feet. Leaves one inch with shallow teeth. Flowers white and fragrant. Berry is dark blue and edible.
Distribution. Grows widely from 2,000 to 9,000 feet on North and South rims and moist places in canyon among pinyon-juniper woodland and coniferous forests.
Remarks. A favorite winter food of deer.

CURLLEAF MOUNTAIN MAHOGANY *(Cercocarpus ledifolius)*

Description. Small, many-branched tree to fifteen feet. Leaves one inch long, narrow with rolled-under margins, leathery and evergreen. Feathery fruit.
Distribution. Grows from 6,000 to 8,800 feet. Typically among pinyon-juniper woodland and ponderosa forests. Grows on North Rim, including Bright Angel Point and Point Imperial, plus Grandview Point on South Rim.
Remarks. A high-protein winter food for deer. Sometimes called buck brush.

LITTLELEAF MOUNTAIN MAHOGANY
(Cercocarpus intricatus)

Description. Small shrub to five feet. Leaves a half inch, dark green, narrow, leathery. Flowers lack petals, but sepals form green tube with pinkish lobes. Feathery fruit. Grayish stems.
Distribution. Common in rocky ledges on both rims and just below.
Remarks. The feathery fruits of mountain mahogany act as a parachute, allowing the pointed seed to land on the ground with tip toward soil. As feather is moistened, it twists, drilling seed into soil.

ALDERLEAF MOUNTAIN MAHOGANY
(Cercocarpus montanus)

Description. Small shrub, usually under six feet tall, but may reach twelve feet in favorable locations. Small, wedge-shaped leaves with blunt teeth on upper margin. Flowers lack petals, but sepals form green tube with pinkish lobes. Fruit is feathery.
Distribution. Dry, sunny locations between 5,000 and 7,000 feet inside canyon among chaparral and pinyon-juniper woodland habitat.
Remarks. Like most mountain mahoganies, the leaves and twigs of this plant are highly favored by deer and elk as winter food.

SHRUB LIVE OAK
(Quercus turbinella)

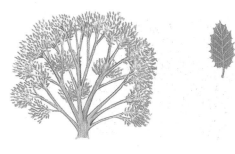

Description. Shrub size with small, shiny, green-blue, hollylike evergreen leaves. Leaves have yellowish, hairy undersides.
Distribution. Chaparral and pinyon-juniper woodlands between 3,000 and 8,000 feet. Found on both rims and within the canyon, including some side canyons like Nankoweap and Kwagunt creeks.
Remarks. Not found along the river below Lees Ferry.

BIG SAGEBRUSH
(Artemisia tridentata)

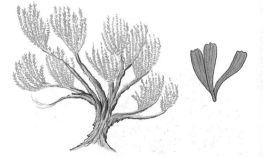

Description. Grayish shrub two to six feet tall. Pungent. Leaves silvery gray-green, long and narrow with three-parted tip. Bark is shredded and gray on older plants.
Distribution. Open flats and slopes or under pinyon-juniper. Common on both rims and Toroweap Valley.
Remarks. An important winter food for mule deer.

FOUR-WING SALTBUSH
(Atriplex canescens)

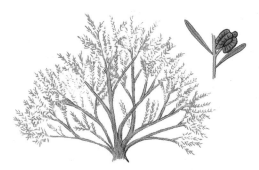

Description. Height two to four feet. Small, densely branched gray-green shrub similar to sagebrush. Produces distinctive light brown, papery four-wing bracts. Leaves are long and narrow, and alternate on each side of branch.
Distribution. Grows from 1,700 feet in bottom of canyon to rims on sandy or salty soils. Found on both sides of the river.
Remarks. Eaten by livestock in winter.

WINTER FAT
(Ceratoides lanata)

Description. Small shrub one to three feet tall. Many erect woolly branches arising from base. Leaves long and narrow, have rolled-under margins, and are densely covered with small hairs.
Distribution. Dry slopes and among grasslands between 1,300 and 6,500 feet. Toroweap Valley, South Rim near Pasture Wash, and within inner gorge.
Remarks. A favorite food of domestic sheep and readily available in winter, hence the name "winter fat."

BANANA YUCCA
(Yucca baccata)

Description. Perennial succulent. Long, linear, stiff leaves with hairs along margin. Creamy flowers on stem in center of plant. Fruit is large, two inches, and oblong.
Distribution. Common from 1,700 to 7,200 feet among pinyon-juniper woodland. Found along Tonto Plateau among blackbrush and on both rims.
Remarks. Pollinated by the yucca moth. Moth cannot reproduce without yucca, since larvae feed upon seeds, but yucca requires moth to be pollinated.

NEW MEXICAN LOCUST
(Robinia neomexicana)

Description. Shrubby, treelike, six to ten feet tall. Leaves are divided into leaflets with nine to twenty-one tiny, opposing leaflets per leaf stalk. At the base of each leaf branch are two stout brown-red one-inch thorns. Fruit is brown, hairy, pealike pod.
Distribution. Grows from 3,000 to 8,500 feet. Common among coniferous forests on both rims, as well in shady canyon locations.
Remarks. Deer and other herbivores eat this plant.

POINTLEAF MANZANITA
(Arctostaphylos pungens)

Description. Grows in brushy clumps three to six feet tall with dense, dark mahogany branches, though branchlets are covered with a grayish, hairy coating. Leaves are longish to oval-shaped with points at the tips, leathery, and bluish green. Berries are reddish brown.
Distribution. Common from 2,500 to 8,500 feet in dry, rocky areas in canyon and rims. Found among chaparral and pinyon-juniper woodlands.
Remarks. A common member of the chaparral community in California, it reaches into Arizona in the Grand Canyon region.

ANTELOPE BRUSH
(Purshia tridentata)

Description. A spreading shrub two to three feet high, grayish green with one-inch wedge-shaped, trident leaves resembling those of sagebrush. The leaf margin is rolled under. Small yellow flowers. The flower capsule has tiny stalked glands on it.
Distribution. Between 5,000 and 7,200 feet in the pinyon-juniper zone.
Remarks. Deer favor the plant for food.

FISH

There is not an overwhelming diversity of fish in Grand Canyon National Park. Except for the Colorado River, fish would not merit discussion. Although a few permanent tributaries like Bright Angel and Havasu creeks always provided habitat for fish, most of the species found in them also are in the main river.

There are eight native fish species in the Colorado River—the humpback chub, speckled dace, flannelmouth sucker, bluehead sucker, roundtail chub, bonytail chub, Colorado squawfish, and razorback sucker. They adapted to the historical conditions on the river, including huge fluctuations in flows, high sediment, and warm temperatures. Because of a variety of factors, including potential competition from introduced fish and flow changes from upstream dam operations, the roundtail chub, bonytail chub, and Colorado squawfish are gone from the river in the canyon. The status of the razorback sucker is uncertain, but it is very rare and may be locally wiped out.

In contrast, introduced fish have grown in numbers as well as distribution. There are fifteen introduced species in the Colorado between Lees Ferry and Lake Mead—the Utah chub, rainbow trout, cutthroat trout, brown trout, brook trout, carp, virgin river spinedace, woundfin, red shiner, fathead minnow, channel catfish, black bullhead, Rio Grande killifish, striped bass, and largemouth bass. Some are very rare and more or less accidental or known from only one or two specimens.

One major factor in the decline of native fish is the effect the Glen Canyon Dam has had upon the river. The Colorado is now colder and clearer, with lower peak flows than the old free-flowing river. Human introductions of exotic species like rainbow trout into tributaries within the park as well as migrants coming from up Lake Mead or fish flushed downstream from Lake Powell also have harmed native fish.

But these changes began long before the dams and reservoirs stilled the flow of the river. Even before the establishment of the park in 1919, the U.S. Forest Service had begun to stock trout in some of the streams flowing off the Kaibab Plateau. Under National Park Service management, trout stocking continued until 1967, when it was ended. During this period, fish were planted in tributary streams such as Bright Angel, Tapeats, Clear, Shinumo, and Garden creeks.

Before 1900, the dominant fish of the river were the flannelmouth sucker, razorback sucker, squawfish, roundtail chub, bonytail chub, and humpback chub. The first species to be introduced were carp and channel catfish. By 1963, when the gates to the Glen Canyon Dam closed, these two species already dominated the fish fauna.

By 1970, when the first comprehensive fish survey of the river in the Grand Canyon was completed, introduced species made up 90 percent of the fish in the Colorado. Rainbow trout is the dominant non-native species in the river, having replaced carp, which once was the most abundant. Rainbows now spawn in major tributaries such as Nankoweap, Clear, Bright Angel, Deer, and Tapeats creeks. Indeed, on Nankoweap Creek, as many as 1,500 trout spawn. This concentration has attracted bald eagles to the site to feed.

Today, only four native species—the humpback chub, speckled dace, bluehead sucker, and flannelmouth sucker—are still found in sizable numbers in the Grand Canyon. There are several reasons. The Colorado never had many native species. Few fish were able to adapt to the harsh environment. The only native predatory fish in this ecosystem was the Colorado River squawfish, which would reach immense size, earning it the nickname "Colorado River salmon."

With only one major predator, native fish had little reason to develop defenses. When predatory fish were introduced into the river, native fish were vulnerable. Today, the striped bass, a migratory and voracious predator stocked in Lake Mead, has worked its way upstream as far as Stone Creek below the Powell Plateau. What effect it will have on the remaining native fish is uncertain.

Species Accounts

COLORADO SQUAWFISH
(Ptychocheilus lucius)

Description. Up to eighty pounds and five feet in length. Slender and pikelike. Snout long and pointed, end of mouth extends back beyond eye. Dark above and light below.
Distribution. An endemic fish of the main river. Gone from the Grand Canyon, though still found in Colorado tributaries above Glen Canyon Dam.
Remarks. Largest member of the minnow family, known as "Colorado River salmon." Last verified record from Grand Canyon was a fish taken in 1972 at Havasu Creek. Endangered.

RAZORBACK SUCKER
(Xyrauchen texanus)

Description. Up to ten pounds and two feet in length. Distinctive razorlike keel on back behind head that looks like a hump, sometimes giving rise to common name "humpback sucker." Dusky olive color on back, yellow-orange belly.
Distribution. Colorado River basin. Probably no longer reproduces in Grand Canyon. May be locally extirpated.
Remarks. Endangered. May live up to fifty years.

FLANNELMOUTH SUCKER
(Catostomus latipinnis)

Description. Up to two feet in length. Long body with large dorsal fin. Large fleshy lobes on mouth. Moderately notched tail. Light gray to greenish, fading to yellow along sides, very pale belly. Underside of head pinkish.
Distribution. Colorado River basin. Found in pools of large rivers and streams.
Remarks. One of the few native fish holding its own in the face of changing river conditions.

BONYTAIL CHUB
(Gila elegans)

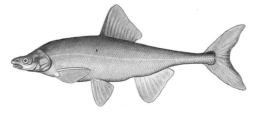

Description. Up to fifteen inches. Sleek with a long, narrow tail. Silver-gray to bluish on back to white or silvery on belly. Breeding males take on an orange-red color over the forward part of body.
Distribution. Colorado River basin. No longer found locally.
Remarks. Endangered.

ROUNDTAIL CHUB
(Gila robusta)

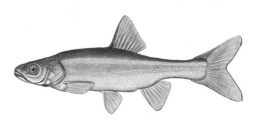

Description: Up to fifteen inches. Broad in middle, tapering to narrow tail. Dark back, silver-gray sides, pale belly.
Distribution. Endemic to the Colorado River system. No longer found in the Grand Canyon.
Remarks. Endangered.

HUMPBACK CHUB
(Gila cypha)

Description. Up to twelve inches. Distinct hump behind head that almost looks like a deformity. Deeply forked tail, sleek overall. Dark back with silvery sides.
Distribution. Once found throughout the Colorado River drainage. A relict group may still live in the Little Colorado River.
Remarks. This fish wasn't even "discovered" by science until 1942, when a visiting scientist found it among a collection in the park archives.

BLUEHEAD SUCKER
(Castostomus discobolus)

Description. Similar to the flannelmouth sucker, except lacks fleshy lips. Tail notched, but less deeply forked than that of flannelmouth sucker.
Distribution. Found in the main river, but spawns in tributaries.
Remarks. As females scoop out spawning nest, they are attended by numerous males that push against the female's body from all sides. As the female releases her eggs, the males release streams of milt, often clouding the water.

SPECKLED DACE
(Rhinichthys osculus)

Description. Length three inches. Rather plain, with light speckles on its sides.
Distribution. Colorado River drainage and all perennial tributaries. Reaches greatest numbers in clear, high-gradient streams like Bright Angel Creek.
Remarks. One of the few native fish that has increased in numbers because of water changes from Glen Canyon Dam. Preferring clear water to the turbid, sediment-laden pre-dam river, the dace has thrived. Nevertheless, it cannot reproduce in cold water and must spawn in warmer tributary streams.

Selected Non-Native Species

RAINBOW TROUT
(Oncorhynchus mykiss)

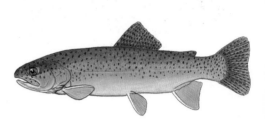

Description. Up to three feet. Olive-green back, pinkish stripe along side, white belly. Black dots over most of upper body. Squarish tail.

Distribution. Clear streams, including the main Colorado below Glen Canyon Dam as well as some tributaries like Nankoweap, Bright Angel, and other creeks.

Remarks. Up to 1,000 or more rainbow trout now spawn in some tributaries. These runs attract bald eagles that winter in the Grand Canyon area. Rainbows are also popular with anglers because of their fighting qualities. A rainbow that weighed over eighteen pounds was caught in the river below Glen Canyon Dam.

BROOK TROUT
(Salvelinus fontinalis)

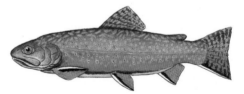

Description. Up to a foot in small streams. Olive-green on back with worm-like black markings. Red spots on sides with blue halos. Belly reddish in breeding males.

Distribution. Cold, clear streams. Has been stocked in tributaries of the Colorado.

Remarks. Not as numerous as the rainbow. State record is a 5.5-pound brook trout taken from Colorado River just below Glen Canyon Dam by Lees Ferry.

BROWN TROUT
(Salmo trutta)

Description. Up to two feet. Olive-brown on back and sides to yellowish on belly. Scatted black and red spots.
Distribution. Main river, some tributaries.
Remarks. Introduced into the United States from Europe.

CHANNEL CATFISH
(Ictalurus punctatus)

Description. Length to two feet or more. Deeply forked tail. Flattened head with many long, black barbels protruding from mouth. Back and sides blue-gray, belly white, often spotted.
Distribution. Native to Mississippi-Missouri river drainage. Now common in Colorado.
Remarks. The most common exotic fish in the river before construction of Glen Canyon Dam. Dozens a day were caught near Lees Ferry.

FATHEAD MINNOW
(Pimephales promelas)

Description. Length two to three inches. Robust body. Blunt, rounded snout and small mouth. Back is tan or olive, sides silvery with dark midline stripe. Belly silvery white.
Distribution. Prefers small, mud-bottom streams. Introduced into Colorado River and tributaries. Especially common in Kanab, Unkar, and Royal Arch creeks. Also in Little Colorado River.
Remarks. Native to streams in eastern United States.

RIO GRANDE KILLIFISH
(*Fundulus zebrinus*)

Description. Length to three inches. Elongated, with distinctive zebralike bars down sides from gills to tail. Back and sides are olive-green, belly silver.
Distribution. Colorado River and tributaries like Kanab Creek and Little Colorado River. Prefers shallow, sandy-bottomed pools and backwaters.
Remarks. Originally native to streams east of the Rockies.

STRIPED BASS
(*Morone saxatilis*)

Description. A large (up to fifty pounds) streamlined silver fish. Large mouth, square tail. Seven or eight black horizontal stripes on sides.
Distribution. Most common in lower parts of the Colorado River within canyon.
Remarks. A saltwater species introduced into Lake Mead in 1969. Also found in Lake Powell. Occasionally moves upstream or downstream from these reservoirs. A voracious predator, this fish could harm other fish species.

CARP
(*Cyprinus carpio*)

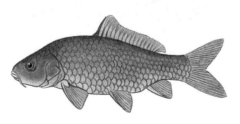

Description. Up to three feet and fifty pounds. Robust, large scales. Two barbels on upper jaw. Back brownish yellow, sides tan, belly lighter. Dark spot at base of each scale.
Distribution. Introduced into Colorado River. Prefers warmer, shallower water.
Remarks. Native to Asia. With the construction of Glen Canyon Dam, carp have declined because of habitat changes; the colder, clear water is less suitable than the old free-flowing river.

AMPHIBIANS AND REPTILES

Grand Canyon National Park offers a wide variety of habitats from desert to subalpine forest. However, the lower elevations of the canyon hold the greatest potential for amphibians and reptiles, since they are cold-blooded and must have warmth for activity.

Not surprisingly, the Grand Canyon is host to far more reptiles and amphibians than parks farther north like Yellowstone or Glacier. According to one estimate, there are fifty-eight species or subspecies that can be found in the park, though some have not been officially documented within its boundaries. Reptiles are better adapted to desert life and are far more abundant in the Grand Canyon area than amphibians.

Amphibians and reptiles include such familiar creatures as snakes, turtles, lizards, toads, salamanders, and frogs. "Amphibian" comes from a Greek word that means "living on both sides of life," referring to the fact that the creature is able to live on land but still is tied to water during some stage of life. Toads, for example, live most of their life on dry land but must lay eggs in water. Reptiles are completely adapted to a land existence, though there are plenty that depend upon watery environments, such as turtles.

In general, amphibians have moist, smooth skin without scales and an aquatic larval stage. Frogs, salamanders, and toads are amphibians. Amphibians breathe through their skin and lungs. Frogs and salamanders must keep their skin moist all the time, so they are rare in the desert; toads are more common. There are fifteen species of toads found in the American deserts, with three in the Grand Canyon.

Reptiles have scaly bodies designed to minimize water loss through their skin. Their shelled eggs enable them to reproduce on land. Snakes, turtles, and lizards are examples of reptiles. They are abundant in desert areas, in part because their activity depends upon temperature. The Grand Canyon's warmth makes reptiles relatively common there. Unlike amphibians, they do not have to return to water to breed and there is no free-living larval stage.

Species Accounts

Salamanders

Salamanders look something like lizards but are amphibians. Like lizards, they are long and thin with long tails. They have smooth, moist skin, no external ears, and no claws. Salamanders are distinguished from frogs and toads because they have a tail throughout their lives. Salamanders vary in color considerably and are very secretive, so they are difficult to identify. They are associated with moist environments and avoid direct sunlight. They eat worms and insects. Typically, they live in damp areas under rocks and logs and prefer cooler temperatures than reptiles, so they are more likely to be observed in the spring and fall.

TIGER SALAMANDER
(Ambystoma tigrinum)

Description. Length 3 to 6.5 inches, not including tail. Tail is oval, flattened toward tip. Broad head, small eyes. Variable color; often glossy gray with smallish black spots, or with brown to black background and cream to yellowish spots that sometimes resemble stripes, hence the name tiger salamander. Young have conspicuous feathery external gills.
Distribution. Widespread in the West. Reported on both sides of the canyon, typically at higher elevations near streams, pools, springs, and water tanks. Occasionally inhabits burrows of ground squirrels or holes in rotten logs, or lives among rocks.
Remarks. Two subspecies are found in the park: Utah tiger salamander (*A. t. utahensis*) and Arizona tiger salamander (*A. t. nebulosum*). Differences are slight. Adults will sometimes migrate to permanent water sources for breeding. Usually only seen on warm nights after rain. The young are called "waterdogs" or axolotl (Spanish for "water lizard").

Frogs and Toads

Adult frogs and toads have powerful back limbs, squat bodies, and lack a tail. In general, toads have warty skin and are oriented toward land, usually lacking webbed feet. Frogs have smooth skin and tend to be more aquatic, usually having webbed feet. There are exceptions, though. Both require water for breeding and produce tailed tadpoles.

Though adult toads are adapted to land, they still require relatively moist air. They are most easily observed after rainstorms, in part because they breathe through their skin as well as their lungs and lose a lot of moisture to dry air. To protect against dehydration, the toad stores water in its bladder; this can make up to 30 percent of its weight. It also can store urea, normally a toxic substance, during dormancy rather than expelling it with water. Toads spend much of their lives hibernating in burrows to avoid extremely cold and dry periods, and this ability is one reason they are relatively successful in arid environments.

Three toad and two frog species are found in Grand Canyon National Park.

ROCKY MOUNTAIN TOAD
(Bufo woodhousei woodhousei)

Description. Length two to four inches. Yellow-brown or grayish with darkish spots above; yellowish and unspotted below. Prominent narrow white stripe down back, distinctive ridges on head between eyes, known as cranial crests. Tips of toes reddish brown. Smoothish skin. Throat patch black in breeding males.
Distribution. Widespread in West, abundant in park. Found at mid-lower elevations in canyon, having been reported at Bright Angel Creek and Phantom Ranch, among other sites.
Remarks. Male has a musical trill call that lasts one to two seconds.

RED-SPOTTED TOAD
(Bufo punctatus)

Description. Length 1.5 to 3 inches. Flattened head and body. Warty skin, greenish or gray with reddish spots and rusty warts. Light undersides. Warts found in front of eyes and on eyelids. Unlike Rocky Mountain toad, red-spotted usually lacks cranial crest.

Distribution. Common in Southwest and most common toad in park. Found at lower elevations along watercourses like Bright Angel Creek, Indian Gardens, and elsewhere.

Remarks. Voice is high, birdlike trill. Breeds from April to July in rocky canyon bottoms with water. Remains in moist crevices and comes out after rains. Only toad that lays eggs one at a time.

GREAT BASIN SPADEFOOT TOAD
(Scaphiopus intermontanus)

Description. Length 1.5 to 2.5 inches. Back is greenish, sides yellowish, with green spots on head and back and light stripes on flanks. Throat and stomach whitish, rear underparts purple. Distinguishing feature is vertical eye pupil, unlike the round pupil of true toads. Spadefoot toads also have relatively smooth skin, lacking warts of true toads.

Distribution. Found widely in Great Basin. Within park it is found on both rims of canyon but is seldom seen, since it remains in burrows much of year.

Remarks. Survives dry seasons by burrowing underground or entering rodent burrows. Sometimes seen during breeding season from April to August, near water sources. The spadefoot has bony appendages on its hind feet that are used to dig out burrows.

CANYON TREE FROG
(Hyla arenicolor)

Description. Length 2 to 2.5 inches. Plump. Looks somewhat like a toad. Gray to dark brown, even black with scattered splotches of dark color on back. Undersides whitish or cream, sometimes orange on the groin. Male has dark throat. No well-defined eye stripe. Long legs and large discs or toe pads for climbing. Most distinctive feature is light spot below eye.
Distribution. Common in Southwest. Within park, most common between mid-elevations and rim. Abundant along streams.
Remarks. Call sounds like a duck or goat. Tends to remain motionless when threatened, relying on camouflage to avoid detection.

LEOPARD FROG
(Rana pipiens)

Description. Length three to four inches. Only frog with randomly distributed dark oval spots above and white underthighs. Smooth skin. Distinctive light-colored ridge on either side of back running from head to tail.
Distribution. Found from Yukon to Arizona. Not common in park; always associated with water.
Remarks. Calls are low, gutteral moans and grunts.

Geckos

Geckos have soft skin, large eyes, and broad-tipped toes. They are good climbers and can cling to the undersides of logs, rocks, and other surfaces as they run. They feed on insects, worms, and spiders. Only one species, the desert banded gecko, is known to inhabit the park, but a subspecies, the Utah banded gecko, may also be found.

DESERT BANDED GECKO
(*Coleonyx variegatus variegatus*)

Description. Length two to three inches. Cream or yellowish above with brown crossbands on body and tail. Undersides whitish and unmarked. Has vertical pupil and distinctive protruding, movable eyelids.

Distribution. Under stones, yucca stems, and other debris in the lower canyon.

Remarks. Can withstand body temperature of just eighty-four degrees, eighteen degrees lower than the preferred temperature of most lizards. This permits geckos to forage at night when other lizards are less active, so they are mostly nocturnal and seldom seen. When stalking prey, waves tail like a cat.

Lizards

Lizards typically have four limbs, a long tail, nonexpandable jaw, ears, eyelids, and scaly skin. They have excellent vision and sense of smell. Most hibernate in colder weather.

ARIZONA NIGHT LIZARD
(*Xantusia vigilis arizonae*)

Description. Length 1.5 to 2 inches, excluding tail. Yellow or grayish above, with spotting. Undersides whitish–pale gray with very light spots.

Distribution. Rare; associated with riparian areas in canyon, particularly around yuccas.

Remarks. Good climber. Can change color depending upon habitat. Subspecies arizonae is largest of the night lizards.

WESTERN CHUCKWALLA
(*Sauromalus obesus obesus*)

Description. Largest lizard in park. Length five to eight inches excluding tail. With tail, may reach eighteen inches. Flattened, plump body. Brownish gray above to white and cream below with dark chest. Markings on back give it a mottled look. Throat has orange or yellow spot. Black markings on each side between limbs. Folds of loose skin by neck. Males tend to have blackish heads and forebodies.
Distribution. Uncommon. Rocky hillsides. Found primarily in Inner Gorge, but occasionally along Redwall Limestone.
Remarks. Tolerates heat better than other reptiles and is often active during the day. A vegetarian, consumes leaves and flower buds. Does not drink; gets all water from food. When vegetation begins to dry out, it cannot flush salts from its body in urine, so excretes them through its nostrils.

ZEBRA-TAILED LIZARD
(*Callisaurus draconoides*)

Description. Length 2.5 to 3.5 inches. Has external ear. Body and tail flattened. Pale gray above with yellowish to whitish spots. Two lines of dark spots on back, with black bands over white on tail. Sides yellowish, fading to whitish. Male has blue patch marked with black bars on belly and sides.
Distribution. Uncommon in side canyons. Sandy and gravelly areas along washes.
Remarks. Fastest lizard, clocked to eighteen miles per hour. When running, lifts front feet off ground and runs on hind legs only.

LONG-NOSED LEOPARD LIZARD
(Gambelia wislizenii)

Description. Length three to five inches. Robust body with large head. Gray or light brown above with many large, dark spots encircled by white dots on body and tail; whitish crossbars on back. Whitish to yellowish below. Can change colors.
Distribution. Rare in park. Associated with desert shrubs.
Remarks. Eats other lizards; will bite if handled.

COLLARED LIZARD
(Crotaphytus collaris baileyi)

Description. Body three to five inches, eight to fourteen inches overall. Large head is distinctive. Tail commonly twice the length of body. Two conspicuous black collars, broken by white-gray area around shoulders. Greenish on spotted back, with dark bands on tail and back. Underparts whitish, tinged with blue. Dark mouth lining.
Distribution. Common in park in dry habitats. Found on both sides of canyon, usually not above 6,000 feet.
Remarks. Agile; will climb shrubs. When chased, lifts up tail and front legs and runs on hind legs.

MOJAVE BLACK-COLLARED LIZARD
(Crotaphytus insularis bicinctores)

Description. Similar to collared lizard. Tan to olive. Conspicuous black and white collar across back of neck. Light-colored mouth lining. Mature male has bluish throat with black center.
Distribution. Inner canyon.
Remarks. Frequently seen basking on rocks.

YELLOW-BACKED SPINY LIZARD
(Sceloporus magister uniformis)

Description. Body three to five inches, excluding tail; up to twelve inches overall. Black wedge-shaped shoulder patch. Skin yellowish tan above with sometimes indistinct crossbands or spots; undersides whitish to pale yellow. Obvious rough, spiny scales along back. Male has blue throat patch. Three lateral stripes on head and neck.
Distribution. Common among yuccas, cacti, small trees, and brush, which it readily climbs. Has been found on South Rim, but more common in mid-lower canyon.
Remarks. Frequents prickly pear cactus, where its tough scales may protect it from thorns. Hunts insects.

NORTHERN PLATEAU LIZARD
(Sceloporus undulatus tristichus)

Description. Body three inches. Tail long. Overall length to eight inches. Mottled dark gray-brown above with a blue wedge-shaped patch on either side of throat. Male has blue underneck and sides. Wavy crossbars on back. Spiny, scaly skin.

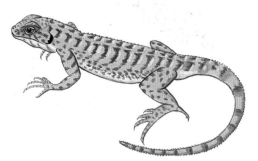

Distribution. Common at higher elevations in park. Found among ponderosa pine, juniper, and sagebrush-grasslands on both rims.

Remarks. Sometimes called eastern fence lizard. Two similar subspecies in park, *S. elongatus* and *S. tristichus*. Fast runner, good climber. Most active on sunny days. Has a breakaway tail: If lizard is attacked, tail breaks off and continues to wiggle, often distracting predator so lizard can escape. Tail is regenerated. In some studies, up to 40 percent of all such lizards had no tails.

NORTHERN SAGEBRUSH LIZARD
(Sceloporus graciosus graciosus)

Description. Body 2 to 2.5 inches; 6 inches with tail. Grayish to olive above. Three faint stripes running down length of back and sides. Black bar on shoulder, solid blue throat, and rusty to yellowish on sides sometimes tinged with blue. White on back of legs. Scaly spines.

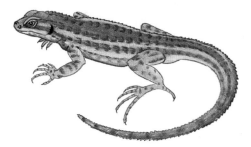

Distribution. Very common on rims, though found in canyon as well. Primarily sagebrush flats, pinyon-juniper, and ponderosa stands. Ground dweller; hides in crevices, rodent burrows. May climb trees.

Remarks. Feeds on grasshoppers and other insects. One of the lizards most likely to be seen by visitors on rims.

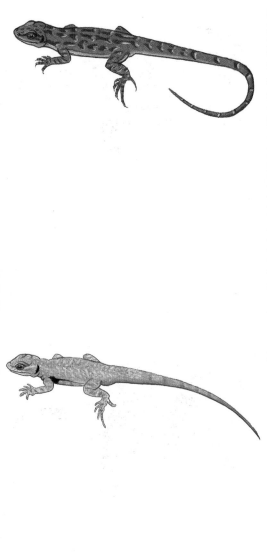

TREE LIZARD
(*Urosaurus ornatus*)

Description. Two to 2.5 inches, to 6 inches with tail. Slender, with an enlarged band of dorsal scales on either side of back separated by central row of smaller scales. Upper body grayish to yellow-brown with herringbone cross-barred back markings. Underparts whitish. Single dark line along sides from head to tail. Males has blue patches on belly, pale blue to yellow throat patch. Female lacks such belly markings and has yellow or orange throat.
Distribution. Common. Riparian zone. Among rocks and trees with shrubby vegetation within the inner canyon.
Remarks. Eats insects. Very good climber. Often seen nimbly running up and down trees and boulders.

SIDE-BLOTCHED LIZARD
(*Uta stansburiana*)

Description. Body length 1.5 to 2 inches, to 7 inches with tail. One of the smallest lizards in park. Brown above with blotches, sometimes blue and yellow speckles. Undersides whitish. Male often has pale blue flecks. Distinctive black spot behind armpit.
Distribution. Common at lower-middle elevations in canyon. Primarily a ground dweller. Prefers sandy soils but found among rocks as well.
Remarks. Two similar subspecies in park, *stejnegeri* and *stansburiana*. Insect eater. Easily loses tail if grabbed by predator. Can regenerate new one.

MOUNTAIN SHORT-HORNED LIZARD
(Phrynosoma douglasii hernandesi)

Description. Body length 2.5 to 4.5 inches. Squat, flattened body with spiny, short, stubby tail. Short, reddish head spines and single row of lateral abdominal spines. Slate gray to light tan. Large, dark blotch on each side of neck. Transverse bars down back.

Distribution. Common among ponderosa and pinyon-juniper on both rims.

Remarks. Only lizard in park to bear live young. Preferred food is ants, which are difficult to digest and of limited nutritional quality. To get enough nutrition, horned lizard must eat a lot of ants; to do so, it has the largest stomach of any desert lizard, making up 13 percent of body.

SOUTHERN DESERT HORNED LIZARD
(Phrynosoma platyrhinos calidiarum)

Description. Body length 2.5 to 4 inches. Squat, flattened body with spiny, short, stubby tail. Short head spines with one row of lateral fringe scales on body, and one row of enlarged scales on each side of throat. Color varies with soil; can be gray, brown, or yellowish. Dark lateral bars or splotches on back.

Distribution. Relatively rare in Grand Canyon; found at lower elevations than the mountain short-horned lizard. Arid regions, generally sandy and gravelly flats among low-growing shrubby vegetation.

Remarks. Are not swift, so they rely on camouflage to avoid predators. Spiny horns make them hard to swallow. They may try to startle a predator by ejecting blood from the corners of their eyes. Able to squirt blood up to six feet.

Whiptails

Whiptails tend to have slender bodies and long tails. They have forked tongues that are often extended beyond the lips. Their movements are jerky. There is only one whiptail species in the park.

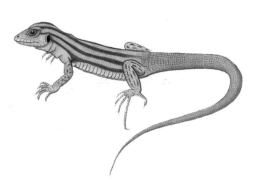

NORTHERN WHIPTAIL
(Cnemidophorus tigris septentrionalis)

Description. Body length three to four inches, up to twelve inches including the long, thin tail. Back has many black or dark brown transverse bars separated by four to six yellowish longitudinal stripes. Upper chest has gray to black spots. Sometimes called tiger lizard because of its stripes. Immature animals have bright blue tails.

Distribution. Lower elevations of canyon. Found in a variety of habitats, including dry washes and rocky areas. Hides in rodent burrows and among brush.

Remarks. Swift but erratic, jerky gait. Starts and stops suddenly. Active hunter, constantly moving from place to place seeking prey. Digs through leaf litter and duff to find moths and butterfly larvae, beetles, and spiders.

Skinks

Skinks are lizards with shiny scales and short legs. Back and belly scales are more or less uniform size. They lay eggs that the female often tends until hatched. They hibernate in winter. Within the Grand Canyon, there are two rarely seen species.

SOUTHERN MANY-LINED SKINK
(Eumeces multivirgatus epipleurotus)

Description. Body two to three inches, up to eight inches with tail. Slender body; short limbs. Pale olive or gray. Numerous stripes cover back and sides. The first and fourth stripes are the widest. Bordered on each side by dark stripe. Underparts generally gray with a cream-colored throat. Immature animals have bright blue tails.
Distribution. Rare; only a few specimens collected. Found in pinyon-juniper forest on South Rim.
Remarks. Secretive.

GREAT BASIN SKINK
(Eumeces skiltonianus utahensis)

Description. Body length 2.5 to 3 inches, up to 9 inches with tail. Dull blue-gray tail in subadults; gray or brown in adults. Four light stripes along back and side to tail. Broad brown band on back between light stripes; broad dark band on sides between light stripes.
Distribution. Rare; found under leaf litter and inside rotten logs. Associated with juniper and ponderosa forests.
Remarks. Secretive. Moves with rapid, snakelike, side-to-side movement.

Gila Monsters

These stout, poisonous lizards have beadlike scales and have venom glands on their lower jaws.

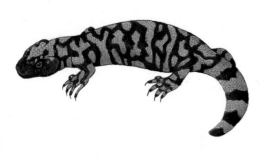

GILA MONSTER
(Heloderma suspectum)

Description. Body length twelve to sixteen inches. Largest lizard in United States. Overall thick, swollen body is distinctive. Tail about one-third length of body. Black and orangish pink irregular splotches or barring. Beadlike skin is most telling characteristic beyond large size.
Distribution. Very rare. Low elevations of western edge of park. Found in desert flats and washes among cactus and creosote bush.
Remarks. Only venomous lizard in the United States. When it bites, the Gila monster chews slowly to pump venom into wound. Venom is neurotoxic and affects respiratory and circulatory systems. Seldom fatal to humans. Feeds primarily on eggs of ground-nesting birds. Stores fat in its thick tail to tide it over during lean periods.

Snakes

Snakes are limbless reptiles. They have no ear openings or movable eyelids. Their jaws are expandable. A snake hears through vibrations picked up by its body from the ground. Several times a year, they cast off their old skins. Snakes are completely carnivorous and may eat up to 50 percent of their body weight in one sitting. Though relatively common, snakes are not often seen in the park because of their shy, primarily nocturnal habits.

WESTERN BLIND SNAKE
(*Leptotyphlops humilis*)

Description. Up to sixteen inches. Almost appears headless. Vestigial eyes are black spots. Dark brown to pink on top, fading to light pink or whitish gray below. Shiny, smooth scales. Tail tipped with small spine.
Distribution. Rare; found in desert shrub in Inner Gorge, under rocks and boulder-strewn slopes.
Remarks. Tends to burrow into loose sand. Occasionally seen at night.

RED RACER SNAKE
(*Masticophis flagellum*)

Description. Length to 100 inches. Slender. Variable color, but often reddish to bluish black. Lacks distinctive patterns. Faint crossbanding, occasionally with lengthwise streaking.
Distribution. Uncommon. Primarily found along the riparian zone of the Colorado River and the lower segments of tributaries.
Remarks. Also called coachwhip snake. Relatively swift. One of the few snakes commonly seen during the day. Consumes prey alive.

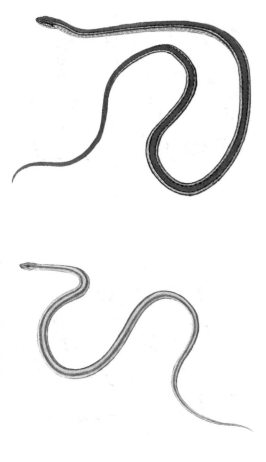

DESERT STRIPED WHIPSNAKE
(*Masticophis taeniatus taeniatus*)

Description. Length to five feet. Long and slender. Head brown above and yellow below. Dark, typically brown or even black with light stripe on each side bisected by darkish line, giving the appearance of several stripes running length of body. Belly is lighter, often yellowish to milky.

Distribution. Common. Lower elevations along rocky, brushy hillsides and stream courses. Observed on both rims.

Remarks. Also called whipsnake. Quick. Will climb trees in search of nesting birds and nestlings.

MOJAVE PATCH-NOSED SNAKE
(*Salvadora hexalepis mojavensis*)

Description. Length up to four feet. Slender body and tail. Light gray above with back stripe that runs from head to tail, sometimes obscure. Top of head brown. Yellowish to whitish below.

Distribution. Uncommon. Low elevation. Brushy desert in canyon.

Remarks. A swift, active snake that is primarily a ground dweller, but will climb shrubs.

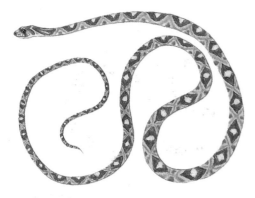

SONORAN LYRE SNAKE
(*Trimorphodon biscutatus lambda*)

Description. Length to three feet. Slender with broad head. Eyes have vertical, elliptical pupils. V-shaped mark on head similar to a lyre, hence name. Blotches on body.

Distribution. Rare in canyon. Found at lower elevations among rocky areas and crevices.

Remarks. Venomous, but poison does not affect humans.

SONORAN GOPHER SNAKE
(Pituophis melanoleucus affinis)

Description. Length to five or six feet. One of the largest snakes in park. Generally light brown or gray above with large oval blotches, checkered sides, and black bar from mouth through eye and across head. Narrow, tapering head. Undersides creamy white.

Distribution. Commonest snake in park. Only found south of river, but in nearly all habitats, including the rim and Tonto Plateau. Likes brush and trees.

Remarks. Will mimic a rattlesnake by vibrating tail, but is not poisonous. Gentle and can be handled easily, one reason they are used in Hopi snake ceremonies.

GREAT BASIN GOPHER SNAKE
(Pituophis melanoleucus deserticola)

Description. Length to six feet. Largest snake in park. Light brown or gray above with dark blotches across back and sides. Black bar from mouth through eye and across head. Undersides whitish to cream.

Distribution. Common. Only found north of Colorado River. Associated with ponderosa forests and grasslands.

Remarks. One of two subspecies of gopher snakes in the park.

UTAH MOUNTAIN KING SNAKE
(Lampropeltis pyromelana infralabialis)

Description. Length up to thirty inches. Light-colored snout (California king snake has black snout), but bright red, black, and creamy bands extend around body. Bands typically alternate between red and white separated by black as follows: red, black, white, black, red, black.

Distribution. Rare. Associated with coniferous forests on North Rim.

Remarks. Similar to coral snake (not found in park) and sometimes called coral king snake. However, king snake's red bands are always between black bands.

CALIFORNIA KING SNAKE
(Lampropeltis getulus)

Description. Length up to four feet. Bold markings. Banded with cream or white alternating with black and red encircling body. Black bands are often widest on upper part of body, while white bands are widest on bottom. Snout is usually black.
Distribution. Common in canyon bottom and some side canyons such as Havasu.
Remarks. Called king snake because it dominates other snakes and will prey on them.

WESTERN LONG-NOSED SNAKE
(Rhinocheilus lecontei lecontei)

Description. Small, not more than two to three feet in length. Tricolored, with cream-colored, pointed snout. Slender black bar or spots below eye on jaw. Back has black banding bordered by white, interspaced with red bands. Belly cream-colored. Scales on underside of tail form single row; most snakes have two rows.
Distribution. Rare. Found in Inner Gorge. Usually associated with rocky habitat, but sometimes burrows into soft sand or soil.
Remarks. Vibrates tail if irritated.

WANDERING GARTER SNAKE
(Thamnophis elegans vagrans)

Description. Length two to three feet. Dark overall, with light yellow stripe along back on either side and lateral stripe on each side. Often has two sets of alternating slate or black spots on either side. Head is distinct from neck, brown above, yellow below.
Distribution. Uncommon. Found on both rims.
Remarks. Bears live young. Has an unpleasant odor.

WESTERN GROUND SNAKE
(Sonora semiannulata gloydi)

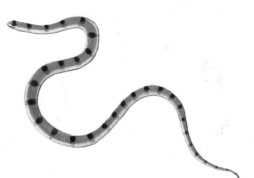

Description. Length usually less than twenty inches. Head only slightly larger than neck. Overall light head with dark bar from eye toward back of neck. Resembles king snake in some ways with conspicuous banding, but only has black and red bands encircling body, though both colors tend to fade toward the belly. Underparts yellowish or light colored.
Distribution. Uncommon. Found in inner canyon and along river, often where there is loose, sandy soil.
Remarks. Not much is known of this snake. Appears to burrow in sandy soil.

NIGHT SNAKE
(Hypsiglena torquata)

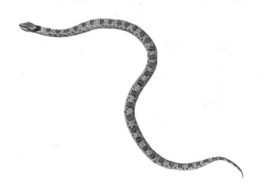

Description. Length one to two feet. Vertical, elliptical pupils. Light brown with brown spots and short, tapering tail. Short, flattened, projecting snout. Distinct black line extends from jaw to eye.
Distribution. Nocturnal, rare. Often hides beneath stones, boulders, and brush. Reported at lower elevations of park.
Remarks. Two similar subspecies, desert night snake *(Hypsiglena torquata deserticola)* and spotted night snake *(Hypsiglena torquata ochrorhynchus)*. Venom is toxic to prey, but reported to be harmless to humans.

UTAH BLACK-HEADED SNAKE
(Tantilla planiceps)

Description. Small, six to fifteen inches. Black cap on head. Usually bordered by white collar on neck. Dull brown color above, orange or red stripe down belly.
Distribution. Rare. Higher elevations on rim among ponderosa and juniper.
Remarks. Tends to burrow. Seldom seen.

SOUTHWESTERN SPECKLED RATTLESNAKE
(Crotalus mitchellii pyrrhus)

Description. Length two to four feet. Triangular head. Pits between nostrils and eyes. Variable color; can be tan, salmon, brown, or light gray. Conspicuously speckled. Blotches on back that sometimes form crossbands. Blotches on sides.
Distribution. Rare. Among desert shrubs.
Remarks. Bears live young. Nervous; rattles when annoyed.

NORTHERN BLACK-TAILED RATTLESNAKE
(Crotalus molossus molossus)

Description. Length two to four feet. Triangular head. Pits between nostrils and eyes. Easily distinguished by solid black tail and black snout. Greenish to yellow-green.
Distribution. Rare. Reaches its northern limits here. Found among juniper.
Remarks. Ground dweller; too heavy to be found among shrubs or trees. Bears live young.

GRAND CANYON RATTLESNAKE
(Crotalus viridis abyssus)

Description. Length up to three feet. Triangular head. Pits between nostrils and eyes. Dirty pink color varying from vermilion to salmon, with body blotches that fade with age.
Distribution. Uncommon in park. Inside the canyon.
Remarks. Only snake endemic to the canyon and only rattlesnake commonly found inside it. Bears live young.

GREAT BASIN RATTLESNAKE
(Crotalus viridis lutosus)

Description. Length to three feet. Triangular head. Pits between nostrils and eyes. Light brown or gray with dark, well-defined blotches that almost appear as rings near tail. Lighter belly.
Distribution. Uncommon in park. Primarily found among ponderosa forests, and only on North Rim.
Remarks. This is the common rattlesnake of the Great Basin region. Bears live young.

HOPI RATTLESNAKE
(Crotalus viridis nuntius)

Description. Length to three feet. Triangular head. Pits between nostrils and eyes. Pinkish to red-brown. Typically the only rattlesnake found on South Rim.
Distribution. Uncommon. Pinyon-juniper forests on South Rim and just below.
Remarks. Rattlesnake used in Hopi snake dance, hence name. Bears live young.

BIRDS

Grand Canyon National Park is home to 315 species of birds, including five exotic ones like the ring-necked pheasant, European starling, and house sparrow. However, many species are migrants or only occasionally recorded.

The variety of habitats is one key in bird identification. Most birds display seasonal preferences. One would not expect to find a black-chinned hummingbird, a creature of the hot desert zone, on top of the Kaibab Plateau in summer. Another hummingbird, the rufous, is relatively abundant among the Kaibab's flowery meadows during late summer. Just knowing the preferred habitat of a species helps to narrow down identification.

There are a number of major ecological zones in the Grand Canyon. Each is broken down into specific plant communities, such as the riparian habitat along the Colorado River. Certain birds are associated with each plant habitat. The following descriptions define each habitat and the species generally associated with it. Few species are restricted to a particular habitat, however.

Lower Sonoran Zone

Riparian Habitat and River Corridor

Riparian areas are the thin, green lines of water-dependent vegetation found along rivers, streams, springs, and seeps. Smaller plants like willow, cattails, and maidenhair fern, as well as trees like salt cedar (tamarisk) and cottonwood, are generally associated with riparian habitat. In the arid West, riparian habitat is rare but biologically critical. Riparian habitat makes up less than 1 percent of the land area but is critical to the survival of 75 to 80 percent of all species.

Waterfowl and shrub-nesting birds are especially attracted to this habitat. In the Grand Canyon, most riparian habitat is found along the Colorado River. There are also a dozen major tributaries that have extensive reaches of riparian habitat.

Since the construction of Glen Canyon Dam, riparian habitat within the Grand Canyon has increased. This does not necessarily mean a net gain to the river corridor, since much riparian habitat was flooded by Lake Powell, which formed behind the dam. Before dam construction, scouring floods were fairly common. Because of recent stable conditions, however, the zone of riparian vegetation has increased.

Among the species commonly associated with riparian habitat are the black-throated blue warbler, lazuli bunting, yellow warbler, black-chinned hummingbird, common yellowthroat, yellow-breasted chat, dipper, black phoebe, spotted sandpiper, Costa's hummingbird, ash-throated flycatcher, violet-green swallow, Bewick's wren, canyon wren, blue-gray gnatcatcher, Bell's vireo, Lucy's warbler, red-winged blackbird, great-tailed grackle, brown-headed cowbird, summer tanager, Bullock's oriole, hooded oriole, blue grosbeak, and lesser goldfinch.

Hot Desert

Immediately beyond the riparian habitat of the Colorado River, between 1,200 and 4,000 feet elevation, lies a zone of plants adapted to hot desert conditions, including barrel cacti, creosote bush, ocotillo, Joshua tree, white bursage, four-winged saltbush, and cholla.

Because of the aridity and lack of plant cover, there are few bird species found in this region. The most abundant are the roadrunner, Say's phoebe, Costa's hummingbird, blue-gray gnatcatcher, black-throated sparrow, and sometimes the cactus wren.

Upper Sonoran Zone

The upper Sonoran zone lies between the Tonto Plateau around 4,000 feet and the rims at 7,000 feet. There are a number of plant communities in this zone, including pinyon-juniper woodland, mountain shrub and chaparral, sagebrush desert, blackbrush desert, and desert grasslands. Each has its own characteristic vegetation and associated bird species.

Desert Grasslands

Desert grasslands are relatively rare in the Grand Canyon region. Native grasses include Indian rice grass, three-awn, and big galleta. The best

Beavertail cacti are common in the inner gorge of the canyon within the hot desert zone, where only a few hardy bird species are abundant.

examples of grasslands are found in the Toroweap Valley and on top of the Grand Wash Cliffs between 3,800 and 5,200 feet.

The birds associated with this habitat are open-country species like meadowlark and horned lark as well as chukar, Brewer's sparrow, and mourning dove.

Blackbrush Desert Shrub

The blackbrush desert shrub community lies in the transition zone from hot desert to cold desert dominated by sagebrush. Blackbrush is the most common plant on the Tonto Plateau within the canyon. Other plants found in limited quantities include prickly pear cactus, cliffrose, rabbitbrush, and acacia.

There are few bird species associated with this habitat. Black-throated sparrows are the most common, plus mourning doves and blue-gray gnatcatchers.

Sagebrush Desert

At a slightly higher, colder elevation is the sagebrush desert. Growing between 4,000 and 7,000 feet, particularly on limestone soils, this plant community is found on the South Rim. It is also common on the Kaibab Plateau and in the Toroweap Valley. Other plants found with sagebrush include four-winged saltbush, snakeweed, banana yucca, and cliffrose.

As with the blackbrush desert shrub community, the black-throated sparrow is the most abundant species. Other birds associated with this type include Brewer's sparrow, mourning dove, and poorwill.

Mountain Shrub and Chaparral

This plant community is often mixed in among the pinyon-juniper woodlands just below the rims. It consists of deciduous species like serviceberry, Gambel oak, skunkbush, snowberry, and fernbush, plus chaparral species like shrub oak, manzanita, and mountain mahogany.

Birds associated with this community include scrub jay, bushtit, black-throated gray warbler, and rufous-sided towhee.

Pinyon-Juniper Woodland

Utah juniper and pinyon pine are the dominant species of this community. This woodland type is common between 4,000 and 7,500 feet elevation. Mixed with these species are others from the mountain shrub and chaparral community like shrub oak, Gambel oak, and mountain mahogany.

Although species diversity is not nearly as great as in the higher-elevation forest communities, there are some birds strongly associated with the pinyon-juniper woodland: black-throated gray warbler, pinyon jay, gray flycatcher, bushtit, plain titmouse, and gray vireo.

Upper-Elevation Forest Zone

The upper-elevation forest zone has two major components: a transition zone dominated by ponderosa forest, and the higher zone of spruce-fir-aspen, sometimes called the boreal zone.

Transition Ponderosa Pine Forest

Ponderosa grows in open parklands between 7,000 and 8,000 feet on large areas of the Kaibab Plateau as well as some of the higher elevations of the South Rim. Other species sometimes found with the pine are Gambel's oak and aspen. On the Kaibab Plateau, white fir is often mixed with ponderosa above 8,000 feet.

Species associated with these woodlands include common flicker, mountain chickadee, Steller's jay, western tanager, acorn woodpecker, solitary vireo, yellow-rumped warbler, Grace's warbler, Virginia's warbler, common nighthawk, pygmy owl, great horned owl, brown creeper, pygmy nuthatch, and white-breasted nuthatch.

Boreal Spruce-Fir-Aspen Forest

The spruce-fir-aspen forest is only found on the Kaibab Plateau above 8,500 feet. This zone is dominated by snowy winters and cool summers. The dominant tree species are Engelmann spruce, subalpine fir, white fir, Douglas fir, and aspen. Lush meadows are interspersed with the trees, providing forest openings.

Bird species in this zone include blue grouse, three-toed woodpecker, ruby-crowned kinglet, warbling vireo, mountain bluebird, hermit thrush, yellow-rumped warbler, Williamson's sapsucker, hairy woodpecker, common flicker, wild turkey, Townsend's solitaire, Clark's nutcracker, and dark-eyed junco.

Species Accounts

The following species accounts do not include every bird found in the canyon area; there are too many to list here. I have featured species that are relatively abundant, hence likely to be encountered, as well as some of the more interesting rare birds. Brief descriptions of each species are provided below to aid in identification, but you should also consult a good field guide. For a complete listing of bird species found in the park and nearby regions, refer to the bird list at the end of this book. For a more complete review, see *Grand Canyon Birds* by Brown, Carothers, and Johnson.

Cormorants

Cormorants are dark birds with long, hooked bills. They dive for fish. Most are seabirds, but one species is found inland.

DOUBLE-CRESTED CORMORANT
(*Phalacrocorax auritus*)

Description. Generally black with yellow-orange throat pouch.
Distribution. Common along the Colorado River in lower canyon. Resident all year, but does not breed.
Remarks. Usually a coastal bird, but now common at Lake Mead, where most of the birds seen in Grand Canyon National Park are assumed to come from.

Herons

Herons are long-legged wading birds with long bills. They often sport long plumes. Six species have been recorded in the park, but only one, the great blue, is common.

GREAT BLUE HERON
(*Ardea herodias*)

Description. Largest heron, four feet tall. Slate gray to bluish with reddish brown neck and black shoulder patches. White head marked by two black plumes. When flying, head is drawn in.
Distribution. Fairly common year-round along river corridor.
Remarks. Transients are sometimes seen in fall at all elevations. Usually nests in colonies.

Swans, Geese, and Ducks

These are web-footed aquatic birds. Although most feed in water, geese will graze. Twenty-seven species have been recorded in the park, but only seven are abundant enough to merit discussion. All recorded species are associated with the Colorado River.

CANADA GOOSE
(Branta canadensis)

Description. Length forty-five inches. Large, gray bird with white cheek patches that stretch from eye to eye under throat; black head, neck, and tail; whitish under-parts.
Distribution. Primarily a winter visitor, common along river. Summer sightings are usually injured birds.
Remarks. Commonly "honks" when in flight.

MALLARD
(Anas platyrhynchos)

Description. Length twenty inches. Males have bright green metallic head and neck. Thin white collar around neck, brown breast, orange feet, yellow bill, gray body. Bright blue speculum feathers bordered by white on wing. Female is generally brown with blue speculum feathers.
Distribution. May be seen year-round, though numbers swell during migration in March and November. Seen wherever there are ponds or open water. Most common along river, particularly during migration, when flocks of 100 are noted.
Remarks. Known to nest in park.

BLUE-WINGED TEAL
(Anas discors)

Description. Length sixteen inches. Male has white crescent just forward of eye, edged by gray below and brown on top of head. White patch forward of dark tail. In both sexes, breast and main body generally brown and speckled. Blue and green patches on wings.
Distribution. Common along river during migrations in spring and fall. Sometimes seen in summer.
Remarks. Known to nest in park.

AMERICAN WIGEON
(Anas americana)

Description. Length eighteen to twenty-three inches. White forehead and metallic green ear patch behind eye. Pale rose-colored breast with white belly.
Distribution. A fall-spring migrant. Usually seen along river.
Remarks. Flies in compact, irregular flocks.

LESSER SCAUP
(Aythya affinis)

Description. Length to sixteen inches. Small, pointed purple head. Black breast, white sides and belly in male. Female is generally brown with white patch in front of bill.
Distribution. Rare in winter, more common during spring and fall migration. Small flocks of ten or so more often seen in flight along rims.
Remarks. Eats primarily aquatic invertebrates and vegetation.

BUFFLEHEAD
(Bucephala albeola)

Description. Length thirteen inches. Small duck. Male with large, puffy white patch on rear top of head. Dark forehead and short bill. White breast and belly. Female with smaller white patch by ear on each side of brown head. Lighter breast and belly.

Distribution. Uncommon winter visitor along Colorado River. Occasionally seen during migration at higher elevations.

Remarks. Mates for long term, strongly tied to breeding areas. When feeding in flocks, one duck usually remains on surface as sentry while others dive.

COMMON MERGANSER
(Mergus merganser)

Description. Length to twenty-five inches. Large duck with long, thin, hooked red-orange bill. Male has dark green metallic head and white breast and belly. In flight, male has white wing patch. Female has rusty head with crest and white chin.

Distribution. A common permanent resident along the Colorado River.

Remarks. Fish eater. Often skitters across water while getting airborne.

American Vultures

These are scavengers with hooked bills and naked heads. They do not build nests but lay eggs on sheltered cliff ledges. Two species have been recorded in the park, but one, the California condor, has not been seen since the late 1800s. Reintroduction to the Grand Canyon is ongoing.

TURKEY VULTURE
(Cathartes aura)

Description. Length to twenty-seven inches. Naked red head, black plumage. Has two-tone wings when seen from below. Wings held upward in shallow V.

Distribution. Common summer resident in all parts of canyon, particularly over open country. Most often seen along rims and cliffs, where updrafts assist in soaring.

Remarks. A carrion feeder, glides over vast areas looking for carcasses. Flocks of forty or more occasionally seen during fall migration.

CALIFORNIA CONDOR
(Gymnogyps californianus)

Description. Length up to 47 inches. Wing span up to 108 inches. Huge size distinctive. Adult has white wing linings set against black. Red, naked head. Flies on flat wings.

Distribution. A former resident in the canyon, now being reintroduced by Marble Canyon.

Remarks. Once found throughout Southwest and Pacific Coast, where it ranged as far north as Oregon. Wild birds ranged over coastal mountains near Santa Barbara, California. Was historically found in region and recorded by two sightings, including one that was shot by Pearce Landing in 1881. By the 1980s, it was nearly extinct. The last wild birds were captured and a breeding program began. Birds raised in captivity are being released into the wild in several locations, including Grand Canyon.

Eagles and Hawks

These are birds of prey with strong talons and bills combined with keen eyesight. They typically have broad wings and tails. Fifteen species are found in the park, but only two are common. Both are soaring types.

The red-tailed hawk is a permanent resident and one of the most abundant raptors in the canyon.

BALD EAGLE
(Haliaeetus leucocephalus)

Description. Length to thirty-seven inches. Adults have white head and tail, brown body, yellow feet, and very large yellow bill. Broad wing span.
Distribution. Seen in winter along Colorado River.
Remarks. A fish eater that has recently been drawn to rainbow trout spawning in Colorado River tributaries.

RED-TAILED HAWK
(Buteo jamaicensis)

Description. Length to twenty-two inches. Most common hawk in region. Light underparts including wings, brown back, and red tail.
Distribution. Permanent resident. Seen throughout the canyon.
Remarks. Will nest on cliffs or trees. Feeds on rodents and rabbits. High number of rabbits in spring ensures greater nesting success in summer.

Falcons

These are sleek, fast birds of prey. They are distinguished from hawks by long, bent wings and longish tails. Four species are found in the park, but only two are common.

AMERICAN KESTREL
(Falco sparverius)

Description. Length to ten inches. Smallest falcon, but most common. Rusty back and tail, gray wings, double black stripes on face. Tends to hover while hunting.
Distribution. Resident along river year-round. Seen elsewhere in park during migrations.
Remarks. Hunts small rodents and insects such as grasshoppers. Nests primarily in old woodpecker holes.

PEREGRINE FALCON
(*Falco peregrinus*)

Description. Length to twenty inches. Black wedge below eye. Black neck and head, whitish throat and chest. Gray back, speckled and streaked belly.
Distribution. Permanent resident, although seldom seen in winter. Associated with cliffs where it nests, and near water like the Colorado River, where it feeds on birds.
Remarks. Endangered by pesticides that caused nesting failure, peregrines are making a slow comeback from the edge of extinction. Prey on white-throated swifts and waterfowl.

Grouse, Turkeys, and Quail

These chickenlike, ground-nesting birds are poor fliers. Five species are found in the park, but only two are discussed here.

WILD TURKEY
(*Meleagris gallopavo*)

Description. Length to forty-seven inches. Large but more slender than domestic turkey. Male has naked blue-red head and wattles on throat. Body metallic brown. Rusty brown tail feathers.
Distribution. Common in ponderosa forests. Found on both rims as well as Mount Trumbull. Occasionally seen below the rims, including Indian Gardens.
Remarks. Turkeys on North Rim and Mount Trumbull were introduced by state game department. Turkeys on South Rim may have been native but also were introduced there in 1946 and 1950.

GAMBEL'S QUAIL
(Lophortyx gambelii)

Description. Grayish above with dark plume feather hanging over face. Males have black face edged by narrow white line, black spot on belly. Females lack black anywhere.

Distribution. Common in desert shrub. Native to canyon, but very local in distribution. Found mostly in western part of canyon, including Toroweap Valley.

Remarks. Edgar Mearns, who recorded wildlife observations during a trip from Ash Fork to the canyon in 1884, noted the birds were abundant during entire journey, including at Havasu Canyon. Less common today.

Wild turkeys are found among ponderosa pine forests on both rims.

Rails, Gallinules, and Coots

These are marsh birds. They typically have short tails and medium-length legs. Since marshes are so rare in the Grand Canyon area, only one species is common.

AMERICAN COOT
(*Fulica americana*)

Description. Length to fifteen inches. Black head and neck, whitish bill with black band near tip. Toes lobed.
Distribution. Common along river in lower portion of canyon near Lake Mead. Rarely seen elsewhere, but have been seen perched in junipers on rim, an unusual position.
Remarks. Paddles along water to get airborne.

Sandpipers and Phalaropes

Shorebirds are most often associated with the ocean. Although sixteen species are found in the park, most are seen only briefly during migration. Only one species, the spotted sandpiper, breeds in the park.

SPOTTED SANDPIPER
(*Actitis macularia*)

Description. Length to seven inches. Brown back, white spotted belly. Smallish, pointed beak. Short tail. White wing stripe visible in flight. Nods and teeters as it walks.
Distribution. Common summer resident. If you see a small shorebird on the beach along the river in summer, it is almost certainly a spotted sandpiper.
Remarks. Only breeding sandpiper in region.

Pigeons and Doves

Most people know the city pigeon. These are plump birds that are strong, fast fliers. Four species are found in the park, but only one is common.

MOURNING DOVE
(*Zenaida macroura*)

Description. Length to twelve inches. Long tapering tail, slim body. In flight, shows white tips on outer tail feathers. Pinkish underparts.
Distribution. Most common summer resident. Found in all habitats. Breeds in all parts of park except high-elevation spruce-fir forest.
Remarks. Call is distinctive *oowoo-woo-woo*. Nests on ground as well as in trees and shrubs.

Owls

These are nighttime birds of prey. Owls have immobile eyes, so they must turn their entire heads to see to either side. Fluffy feathers aid in soundless flight. They find prey through their sense of hearing. There were eight species in the park, but one, the burrowing owl, is no longer found. Only two species are common.

FLAMMULATED OWL
(*Otus flammeolus*)

Description. Length to seven inches. Dark eyes, small ear tufts. Grayish red plumage, streaked and variegated.
Distribution. Especially common in ponderosa pine forests.
Remarks. Depends on holes in old-growth trees for nesting space. Has declined throughout much of its range outside the park as large pines have been cut for timber.

GREAT HORNED OWL
(Bubo virginianus)

Description. Length up to twenty-two inches. Large bird with ear tufts. Brown over most of back, with lighter belly. White throat.
Distribution. Most common in timbered draws and woodlands just below the rims.
Remarks. Most common owl in Grand Canyon and only one that makes the classic *hoot-hoot* call.

Goatsuckers

These are insect-hunting birds of the evening. They roost during the day, usually on the ground. Four species are found in the park, but only two are common.

COMMON NIGHTHAWK
(Chordeiles minor)

Description. Length to nine inches. Grayish brown with long, pointed wings that have white bars near tip. White throat patch.
Distribution. Common throughout higher elevations, particularly plateaus.
Remarks. During courtship flights, male dives and creates a resonating booming sound.

COMMON POORWILL
(Phalaenoptilus nuttallii)

Description. Length to eight inches. Short, rounded tail tipped in white. Broad white patch crosses throat. Overall color is mottled brown-gray.
Distribution. Common summer resident of mid-elevation rocky slopes of canyon. Found on Tonto Plateau or among juniper-pinyon woodlands.
Remarks. Will hibernate in colder weather.

Swifts

These are fast-flying birds with long, curved wings and short tails. They feed on insects. Only one species is found in the park.

WHITE-THROATED SWIFT
(Aeronautes saxatalis)

Description. Length to seven inches. Long, pointed wings, forked tail. Black back, white chest and belly, black along sides.
Distribution. Common summer resident in canyons and cliffs, where it nests in crevices.
Remarks. Has weak legs, so it does everything on the wing, including eating, drinking, and even mating. Swifts are a major food of the endangered peregrine falcon.

Hummingbirds

These are tiny nectar-feeding birds that hover. They can be very aggressive. Their wing whir sounds like a large bee buzzing. Seven species have been found in the park; the four most common are discussed below.

BLACK-CHINNED HUMMINGBIRD
(Archilochus alexandri)

Description. Length nearly four inches. Metallic green on back. Male has black throat with metallic violet band immediately above white chest. Female has nearly all white undersides.
Distribution. Lowlands. Abundant during summer in low parts of canyon, particularly riparian zone. Also seen occasionally among pines and juniper forests on rims.
Remarks. Most common breeding bird in river corridor; nests primarily in an introduced tree, the salt cedar.

COSTA'S HUMMINGBIRD
(Calypte costae)

Description. Length to 3.5 inches. Metallic green back, violet head and throat in males. Whitish belly.

Distribution. Common in desert washes. In canyon, prefers lowest, driest habitat. Common summer resident of the desert shrub habitat with ocotillo and creosote bush.

Remarks. Was thought to be rare, though it is relatively common along lower river corridor. However, it breeds in April and May, before most river runners arrive, so few canyon visitors see this bird when it is most abundant.

BROAD-TAILED HUMMINGBIRD
(Selasphorus platycercus)

Description. Length to four inches. Metallic green on back. Male has reddish throat, white chest and belly, green patch below white on sides. Female lacks red throat patch.

Distribution. Common summer resident of forests. Most abundant in spruce-fir forests of Kaibab Plateau.

Remarks. Tips of male's primary wing feathers are notched. Air passes rapidly through them, producing a high whirring noise—a key characteristic of this bird.

RUFOUS HUMMINGBIRD
(Selasphorus rufus)

Description. Length to four inches. Named for its rufous (reddish) tail. Male has reddish back, green crown.
Distribution. Breeds in Pacific Northwest, but migrates to seek blossoms at higher elevations, following chain of mountains along spine of Rockies. Common along the Kaibab Plateau, particularly in later summer and early fall.
Remarks. During height of migration, rufous hummingbirds outnumber resident broad-tails, competing for access to favorite flower patches.

Kingfishers

Large head, crest feathers, and short legs identify this fish-eating bird of creeks and rivers. One species is found in the park.

BELTED KINGFISHER
(Ceryle alcyon)

Description. Length to thirteen inches. Stocky, short-legged. Crested, pointed bill, bluish gray plumage on back, blue breast band. White belly.
Distribution. Feeds on fish, so found near water. Does not breed in canyon, so most often seen during spring and fall migrations.
Remarks. Vernon Bailey, a famous biologist who wrote early reports on the Grand Canyon's birds, reported seeing a kingfisher digging a hole along Bright Angel Creek in 1929. Since kingfishers nest in burrows, he may have been observing nesting behavior.

Woodpeckers

These are insect-feeding, cavity-nesting birds with stiff tail feathers, short legs, and strong bills for drilling holes. Twelve species have been found in the park, but only three are discussed here.

RED-NAPED SAPSUCKER
(Sphyrapicus nuchalis)

Description. Length to 8.5 inches. Male has red crown, nape, and throat, with black and white markings on rest of head. Black chest patch, yellow belly, black and white back and wings.

Distribution. Common among aspen groves, so abundant on Kaibab Plateau and Mount Trumbull areas. Found year-round in park, but more common in river corridor and among pinyon-juniper in winter.

Remarks. Until recently considered a subspecies of yellow-bellied sapsucker.

HAIRY WOODPECKER
(Picoides villosus)

Description. Length to nine inches. Red patch on back of black and white head, white back and belly, black elsewhere. Downy woodpecker is similar but smaller. Hairy is larger and has larger, longer bill.

Distribution. Permanent resident of woodlands. Found primarily in ponderosa forests but ranges throughout the canyon. Occasionally found among cottonwoods along river corridor and tributaries.

Remarks. Female watches eggs during day; male sits on them at night. Males tend to forage farther afield while female stays within hearing distance of nest.

NORTHERN FLICKER
(Colaptes auratus)

Description. Length to twelve inches. Relatively large. Brown, barred back with spotted underparts. Black bib.
Distribution. Forested areas on rims and woodlands below. Most common on Kaibab Plateau. Occasionally seen along river corridor in spring and fall.
Remarks. Ants are a major food. There were once three subspecies of the flicker in park: red-shafted (most often seen at Grand Canyon), yellow-shafted (occasionally seen), and gilded (common in Southwest). All are now considered subspecies of the same species.

Flycatchers

Many species of flycatchers are similar and difficult to distinguish. These birds often fly from their perch to grab insects from the air. Fifteen species have been found in the park, but only six are common enough to discuss.

WESTERN WOOD-PEWEE
(Contopus sordidulus)

Description. Length to six inches. Variable plumage, generally dusky gray-green with dullish white throat. Wing bars whitish. Dark tail.
Distribution. Open woodlands. Summer resident in ponderosa forest on rim. Seen in lower elevations during rest of year, except during winter, when it migrates southward.
Remarks. Feeds on insects.

GRAY FLYCATCHER
(*Empidonax wrightii*)

Description. Length to six inches. Gray above, sometimes fading to olive. Whitish below, sometimes pale yellow. Sometimes has pale white eye ring.
Distribution. Sagebrush-juniper or ponderosa forests; has been seen during migrations at other elevations.
Remarks. Gray flycatcher is one of five empidonax flycatchers that are very difficult to tell apart. Similar species are occasionally reported in park, so positive identification is tricky.

BLACK PHOEBE
(*Sayornis nigricans*)

Description. Black head, back, and chest with white belly.
Distribution. Prefers to nest near water. Common summer resident of riparian areas. Resident during winter along river.
Remarks. Uses mud in nest construction. Since closure of Glen Canyon Dam, mud is rarer in canyon, so now most nest sites are in or near tributaries.

SAY'S PHOEBE
(*Sayornis saya*)

Description. Grayish brown above, pale gray throat, tan belly, blackish tail.
Distribution. Prefers dry, open canyons. Common in summer along river, occasionally found elsewhere in canyon. Seldom encountered on forested areas of rim. Winters in river corridor.
Remarks. Frequently hovers just above water as it feeds.

ASH-THROATED FLYCATCHER
(Myiarchus cinerascens)

Description. Length to 8.5 inches. Gray above, gray head, pale chest, yellowish belly, brownish red tail.
Distribution. Throughout canyon, including juniper and ponderosa forests. In river corridor as well.
Remarks. Cavity nester, so associated with trees.

CASSIN'S KINGBIRD
(Tyrannus vociferans)

Description. Length to nine inches. Dark gray back, pale gray chest, yellow belly.
Distribution. Widespread in canyon except for highest coniferous forests. Most common in juniper-pinyon woodlands.
Remarks. Insect eater.

Larks

These are ground-dwelling birds of open fields. They walk rather than hop. Only one species is found in the park.

HORNED LARK
(Eremophila alpestris)

Description. Length to seven inches. Yellowish to white face, black horns, black stripe across chest. Brown back, light belly.
Distribution. Common in grasslands, particularly Toroweap Valley. Occasionally seen in flocks in grasslands on Kaibab Plateau in late summer.
Remarks. Male has elaborate courtship ritual. Will climb to 800 feet, then fold wings and dive steeply.

Swallows

These insect feeders catch prey on the wing. They have slender bodies and long, pointed wings. Seven species have been found in the park, but only two are common.

VIOLET-GREEN SWALLOW
(Tachycineta thalassina)

Description. Dark, glossy, green back with dark head, white behind eye and down throat, chest, and belly. White patches extend up from sides toward rump.
Distribution. Along river corridor and in pine forests on rims. Nests in tree cavities and among cliffs along river.
Remarks. A favored food of the peregrine falcon.

NORTHERN ROUGH-WINGED SWALLOW
(Stelgidopteryx serripennis)

Description. Length up to six inches. White belly, dark brown back.
Distribution. Common in summer along river corridor, where it may nest in cliffs. Seen elsewhere in canyon at other times.
Remarks. Unlike other swallows, this one is more likely to be found as solitary pair rather than in breeding colonies.

Jays, Magpies, and Crows

These are intelligent, aggressive birds with loud calls. Five species are found in the park.

STELLER'S JAY
(Cyanocitta stelleri)

Description. Length to eleven inches. Bright blue, black crest, blackish cast about head and throat.
Distribution. Common in ponderosa pine woodlands. Also associated with oaks. Tames easily, often seen about campgrounds.
Remarks. Bold and aggressive bird.

SCRUB JAY
(Aphelocoma coerulescens)

Description. Length to twelve inches. Long blue tail, blue-gray back, blue head and wings. White belly and chest, gray-brown patch in center of chest.
Distribution. Common in shrublands such as juniper-pinyon woodlands. Occasionally found in canyon at Indian Gardens and elsewhere.
Remarks. Forms long-term pairs; groups remain year-round on territory.

PINYON JAY
(Gymnorhinus cyanocephalus)

Description. Length to 10.5 inches. Blue overall with streaked throat. Short tail.
Distribution. Common in pinyon-juniper woodlands.
Remarks. Colonial. Forms large foraging flocks that wander widely.

CLARK'S NUTCRACKER
(*Nucifraga columbiana*)

Description. Length to twelve inches. Stocky and gray; black wings set off by white patches and white outer tail feathers that can be seen in flight.
Distribution. Common in coniferous forests. Year-round residents of Kaibab Plateau spruce-fir forests. Occasionally seen at South Rim among the ponderosa pine by Grandview Point.
Remarks. Often breeds early while snow is still on ground. Caches seeds from pines on south-facing slopes; must recover them during winter and spring to survive. Each bird must remember up to 1,000 caches each year.

Raven. If you see a large black bird gliding along the canyon rims, most likely you're seeing a raven. Ravens are among the most intelligent of birds and have specific calls used to communicate with other "friends."

COMMON RAVEN
(Corvus corax)

Description. Length to twenty-four inches. Large, black bird with stout black bill, wedge-shaped tail.
Distribution. Found from river to rims. Often seen soaring about rims.
Remarks. Ravens along river preside over campsites, raiding unattended goodies. In winter, sometimes found in communal roosts, with one record of more than 800 ravens.

Titmice

There are three species of these active, agile, small birds in the park, but only two are common.

MOUNTAIN CHICKADEE
(Parus gambeli)

Description. Length to five inches. Small, active, gray bird with black throat bib, black cap, eye patch with white line above eye.
Distribution. Common permanent resident of forested areas, particularly on Kaibab Plateau. Occasionally found as low as pinyon-juniper zone. One of the more common birds along rims in winter.
Remarks. Relies upon abandoned woodpecker holes for nesting.

PLAIN TITMOUSE
(Parus inornatus)

Description. Length to six inches. Small, drab, gray. Small crest on head.
Distribution. Common permanent resident of pinyon-juniper woodlands.
Remarks. Pair often remains together. Cavity nester.

Bushtits

These are similar to chickadees but with a longer tail.

BUSHTIT
(Psaltriparus minimus)

Description. Length to 4.5 inches. Small, nondescript bird, pale gray breast and belly.

Distribution. Woodlands. Permanent resident of pinyon-juniper and chaparral. Abundant along river corridor in winter.

Remarks. Bird weighs little but has large body surface area, so heat loss is a major problem. Bushtits will roost together in tight masses to conserve energy.

Nuthatches

These forage for insects on trees, climbing up and down boles. They have a loud, hornlike call. Three species are found in the park; two are discussed.

WHITE-BREASTED NUTHATCH
(Sitta carolinensis)

Description. Length to six inches. Gray-blue back, black cap, white breast, throat, and belly.

Distribution. Common permanent resident of forests and wooded areas on rims and Kaibab Plateau.

Remarks. Pairs maintain feeding territories throughout year.

PYGMY NUTHATCH
(Sitta pygmaea)

Description. Length to 4.5 inches. Blue-gray back, brownish cap, white throat, tan belly.

Distribution. Common permanent resident in ponderosa forest and occasionally in pinyon-juniper woodlands.

Remarks. Typically nests in old woodpecker holes. Forms breeding units of up to five birds. Like wolf pack members, young of the previous year help adults raise younger siblings.

Creepers

These are small insect-feeding birds with curved bills used to capture prey from beneath tree bark. One species is discussed.

BROWN CREEPER
(Certhia americana)

Description. Length to five inches. Streaked brown back, stiff tail, white throat, breast, and belly.

Distribution. Common summer resident of spruce-fir-aspen forest on the Kaibab Plateau. Moves to ponderosa and juniper woodlands in fall and winter.

Remarks. Eats insects and larvae under bark. Spirals up tree, then flies to next tree and starts at bottom, working up again.

Wrens

Wrens are chunky, smallish birds with slender bills. They often have a distinctive and lovely song. Seven species are found in the park; four are discussed.

ROCK WREN
(Salpinctes obsoletus)

Description. Length to six inches. Gray-brown above with rusty red rump. White, lightly streaked breast. Black tail band, sometimes indistinct.

Distribution. Common around ledges and cliffs. Found throughout the canyon in summer. During winter, moves to river corridor and inner canyon.

Remarks. Lays path of small stones leading to nest entrance.

CANYON WREN
(Catherpes mexicanus)

Description. Length to six inches. White throat and breast, chestnut belly, brown-streaked back.

Distribution. Common in canyons near cliffs. Permanent resident.

Remarks. Loud, distinctive song like a descending trill.

BEWICK'S WREN
(Thryomanes bewickii)

Description. Length to six inches. Grayish back, white underparts, white eye stripe from bill through eye and beyond. Long tail edged in white spots.

Distribution. Permanent resident of river corridor in riparian habitat, as well as dense pinyon-juniper stands on or near rims.

Remarks. Males sometimes build crude "dummy" nests.

HOUSE WREN
(Troglodytes aedon)

Description. Length to five inches. Looks like a larger winter wren with a slightly longer tail. Overall brown body, pale whitish underside.

Distribution. Common summer resident of forests on Kaibab Plateau, though occasionally found just below South Rim among fir and pine.

Remarks. Males sometimes build "dummy" nests. Strong fidelity to breeding territory.

Dippers

This is a chunky, small bird with a short tail that feeds on underwater insects. It swims or walks in mountain streams.

AMERICAN DIPPER
(Cinclus mexicanus)

Description. Length to eight inches. Stocky, gray bird with short tail and wings.

Distribution. Always associated with rushing tributaries of the Colorado River. Nests along Bright Angel, Havasu, Clear, and Tapeats creeks, among others.

Remarks. Related to wrens but favors a watery environment. Dives and swims upstream underwater or walks on bottom, feeding on aquatic insects. Has beautiful, wrenlike song.

Kinglets, Gnatcatchers, Solitaires, and Thrushes

These are woodland birds. Many have beautiful songs and are well known. Seven of the eleven species found in the park are discussed below.

RUBY-CROWNED KINGLET
(Regulus calendula)

Description. Length to 4.5 inches. Small, plump; greenish gray with red crown, two white wing bars, dull whitish gray underparts.
Distribution. A summer resident of spruce-fir forest on Kaibab Plateau. Winters at lower elevations along river.
Remarks. One of the more common birds along the river corridor in winter.

BLUE-GRAY GNATCATCHER
(Polioptila caerulea)

Description. Length to 4.5 inches. Blue-gray above, white below, white-edged black tail. Female is light gray.
Distribution. Common in woodlands and thickets, particularly in riparian areas as well as in denser pinyon-juniper woodlands.
Remarks. Extremely active. Tail is always flicking nervously.

WESTERN BLUEBIRD
(Sialia mexicana)

Description. Length to seven inches. Male's back, wings, shoulders, and head rich blue, with rusty red breast, white belly. Female has grayish head, blue tint to wings, rusty red breast, white belly. Both sexes sometimes chestnut on shoulders and back.

Distribution. Common summer resident of ponderosa and pinyon-juniper woodlands on or near rims. Nests in cavities. Spring transients sometimes found in canyon at lower elevations.

Remarks. This beautiful bird is declining over much of its range as old-growth habitat, necessary for nesting, is cut.

MOUNTAIN BLUEBIRD
(Sialia currucoides)

Description. Length to seven inches. Male rich blue above, paler blue below, with whitish belly. Female grayish with blue tint to wings.

Distribution. Summers on Kaibab Plateau, where it often nests in snags on edge of meadows.

Remarks. Sometimes hovers over meadows while catching insects. Among the many species that benefit from natural events (such as fire, disease, and insect attacks) that create snags.

TOWNSEND'S SOLITAIRE
(Myadestes townsendi)

Description. Length to eight inches. Looks like a gray robin. White eye ring, white outer tail feathers that can be seen in flight.

Distribution. Common summer resident of forested highlands on both rims and Mount Trumbull. Associated with ponderosa pine and spruce-fir forests.

Remarks. Winter food is almost exclusively berries.

HERMIT THRUSH
(Catharus guttatus)

Description. Length to seven inches. Grayish brown back, reddish tail, spotted whitish breast.
Distribution. Common summer resident of spruce-fir forests on Kaibab Plateau. Occasionally sighted among the lower-elevation ponderosa. Prefers moist areas.
Remarks. Song is flutelike.

AMERICAN ROBIN
(Turdus migratorius)

Description. Length to ten inches. Red breast, dark head, brown back.
Distribution. Common summer resident of ponderosa and pinyon-juniper forests.
Remarks. Sometimes produces two broods a year; male cares for first while female incubates second.

Vireos

These are small songbirds with short bills and dull coloration. Six species are found, with three common in the park.

BELL'S VIREO
(Vireo bellii)

Description. Length to five inches. Chunky; olive green back with yellowish underparts. Longish tail. Faint wing bar. Nervous behavior.
Distribution. Common summer resident among dense riparian vegetation along Colorado River.
Remarks. Numbers have increased and range has expanded upstream with construction of Glen Canyon Dam, which has created new high-water vegetation zone.

SOLITARY VIREO
(Vireo solitarius)

Description. Length to 5.5 inches. Grayish back, pale gray breast fading to white belly. Prominent eye stripe and ring. White wing bars.
Distribution. Common in ponderosa and oak woodlands in summer.
Remarks. Frequent target of cowbird, which lays egg in vireo nest. Vireo raises cowbird as its own, to the detriment of vireo's own young.

WARBLING VIREO
(Vireo gilvus)

Description. Length to 5.5 inches. Grayish green on back, yellowish flanks, white breast. Light eye line. Lacks wing bars.
Distribution. Very common summer resident among the spruce-fir-aspen forests on Kaibab Plateau. Also found in ponderosa and oak woodlands.
Remarks. Prefers aspens and oaks for nesting. Like the solitary vireo, suffers from cowbird parasitism.

Wood Warblers

These are small, insect-feeding birds, typically associated with denser vegetation. Twenty-nine species are found in the park; nine are discussed below.

VIRGINIA'S WARBLER
(Vermivora virginiae)

Description. Length to five inches. White eye ring, grayish back, yellowish breast and undertail coverts, white belly.
Distribution. Common in pinyon-juniper woodlands and ponderosa-Douglas fir forests on canyon rims.
Remarks. Often wags tail.

LUCY'S WARBLER
(Vermivora luciae)

Description. Length to four inches. Gray above, pale gray below. Males also have chestnut rump patch and crown.
Distribution. Common summer resident along low-elevation watercourses and riparian zone.
Remarks. One of two North American warblers that nest in cavities.

YELLOW WARBLER
(Dendroica petechia)

Description. Length to five inches. Dark eye, yellow cast overall, with streaked breast on male.
Distribution. Common summer resident in streamside riparian vegetation along river and tributaries.
Remarks. Nests in salt cedar. One of four warblers that breed along Colorado River.

YELLOW-RUMPED WARBLER
(Dendroica coronata)

Description. Length to five inches. Yellow rump, crown, throat; yellow patch by wing, white belly, black to gray over remainder of body except for whitish bars on wings.
Distribution. Common summer resident in spruce-fir forests on Kaibab Plateau. Occasionally found among coniferous forests just under South Rim and on Mount Trumbull.
Remarks. One of the most gregarious of warblers.

BLACK-THROATED GRAY WARBLER
(Dendroica nigrescens)

Description. Length to five inches. Looks something like chickadee. Gray to black over back, head, and chest; two white stripes on face, white belly.
Distribution. Common summer resident in oak-pine-juniper woodlands. More open forests with shrubs.
Remarks. Like most warblers, this bird eats insects.

GRACE'S WARBLER
(Dendroica graciae)

Description. Length to five inches. Gray back, yellow throat and breast, white belly, two white wing bars, yellow eye stripe that turns to white beyond eye. Black streaks on side.
Distribution. Common summer resident of ponderosa forests. Also found among spruce-fir forest on Kaibab Plateau.
Remarks. Typically remains high in trees, foraging on insects. Will capture insects on the wing.

COMMON YELLOWTHROAT
(Geothlypis trichas)

Description. Length to five inches. Male has distinctive black mask. Yellow underparts, olive-gray back. Female lacks mask.
Distribution. Common summer resident of dense riparian vegetation along river corridor, particularly areas with reeds and marsh habitat such as Marble Canyon. During migration, is sighted on both rims.
Remarks. One of the most common warblers. Frequent cowbird host.

WILSON'S WARBLER
(*Wilsonia pusilla*)

Description. Length to five inches. Olive above, yellow below. Male has round black cap. Long, dark tail.
Distribution. Prefers dense vegetation in moist areas. A migrant in canyon during spring and fall. Often seen along river corridor.
Remarks. Color varies geographically.

YELLOW-BREASTED CHAT
(*Icteria virens*)

Description. Length to 7.5 inches. Largest warbler. Generally grayish black with long tail, yellow breast and throat, whitish belly, white eye ring, two white stripes on face by bill.
Distribution. Prefers dense riparian vegetation. Common summer resident along river and perennially flowing tributaries.
Remarks. Secretive; seldom seen.

Tanagers

These are birds of tropical origins, so they are often brilliantly colored. Four species are found in the park; one is common.

WESTERN TANAGER
(*Piranga ludoviciana*)

Description. Length to seven inches. Red head, yellow chest and belly, black wings, yellow wing bars.
Distribution. Common summer resident among coniferous forests on both rims and Mount Trumbull.
Remarks. Winters in Mexico and Central America.

Grosbeaks and Allies

A strong, conical bill for seed crushing is common among these species. Seven are found in the park; three are common.

BLACK-HEADED GROSBEAK
(Pheucticus melanocephalus)

Description. Length to eight inches. Large bill for crushing seeds. Male has reddish underparts, black head, white wing bars on black wings, yellow underwings visible in flight. Female has brown-tan back, pale underparts, white stripe above eye.
Distribution. Common summer resident in woodlands dominated by ponderosa and pinyon-juniper.
Remarks. Occasionally sings while sitting on nest.

BLUE GROSBEAK
(Guiraca caerulea)

Description. Length to seven inches. Sky blue, rusty wing bars, black about eye and bill. Large, heavy bill.
Distribution. Common summer resident of riparian zone. Seen elsewhere in canyon during migration.
Remarks. With its all-blue body, blue grosbeak looks something like indigo bunting, but more robust.

LAZULI BUNTING
(Passerina amoena)

Description. Length to 5.5 inches. Turquoise with cinnamon chest, white belly, white wing bars on darker wings. Female less colorful grayish blue.
Distribution. Prefers brushy areas near water. Common summer resident in riparian vegetation.
Remarks. Forms flocks after breeding and moves to higher elevations

Towhees, Sparrows, and Juncos

This is a large, diverse group of songbirds. Most sparrows are streaked brown above. Towhees are ground-foraging birds. Twenty-five species of this group are found in the park; eight are discussed.

GREEN-TAILED TOWHEE
(Pipilo chlorurus)

Description. Length to seven inches. Reddish crown, olive back, dark brown tail. Gray on face and chest, white throat and belly.

Distribution. Prefers dense, brushy habitat. Common summer resident among spruce-fir forest on Kaibab Plateau, where it typically nests on ground.

Remarks. Often seen scratching away leaf litter looking for seeds and berries.

RUFOUS-SIDED TOWHEE
(Pipilo erythrophthalmus)

Description. Length to 8.5 inches. Male has black head, back, and tail. White spots on shoulders, white wing bars, white outer feathers on tail. Rufous sides, white belly.

Distribution. Prefers dense, shrubby vegetation. Most likely encountered among shrubby oak and chaparral below rims.

Remarks. Nests on ground. Forages by scratching away leaf litter using both feet simultaneously.

CHIPPING SPARROW
(Spizella passerina)

Description. Length to 5.5 inches. Brownish back and crown; pale gray throat, chest, and belly. Dark, thin stripe through eye bordered by thicker white line above. Gray ear patch and neck.
Distribution. Prefers ponderosa forest, but also found among pinyon-juniper on both rims and just below.
Remarks. Often forms small foraging flocks in winter.

LARK SPARROW
(Chondestes grammacus)

Description. Length to 6.5 inches. Head has russet patches separated by white and thin black stripes. White underparts have black spot. Brown back. Outer tail feathers white.
Distribution. Summer resident of grasslands on rims, Toroweap Valley, and inside canyon.
Remarks. Feeds in flocks, even during breeding season.

BLACK-THROATED SPARROW
(Amphispiza bilineata)

Description. Length to 5.5 inches. Black throat and chest surrounded by white belly. White eyebrow. Streaked brown back.
Distribution. Prefers rocky desert slopes. Only breeding bird found among blackbrush on Tonto Plateau. Also seen among big sagebrush on rims. More widespread during migrations.
Remarks. A true desert bird. Appears to be able to survive without drinking, obtaining sufficient moisture from its food, including vegetation and juicy insects.

SONG SPARROW
(Melospiza melodia)

Description. Length to six inches. Long, rounded tail. Generally brown back; dark stripe borders throat. Streaked chest and dark spot in center often visible; otherwise light underparts.
Distribution. Prefers brushy streamside areas. Found on Havasu Creek and riparian areas along river.
Remarks. Most variable North American bird; more than thirty subspecies.

WHITE-CROWNED SPARROW
(Zonotrichia leucophrys)

Description. Length to seven inches. Black-and-white-striped crown. Gray nape and chest, whitish underparts. Brown-streaked back.
Distribution. Prefers open landscapes. Breeds primarily north of Arizona but winters in canyon. Often found at lower elevations fall, winter, and spring.
Remarks. Winter flocks often strongly territorial.

DARK-EYED JUNCO
(Junco hyemalis)

Description. Length to six inches. Gray head, rufous back and sides, white underbelly. White outer tail feathers conspicuous in flight.
Distribution. Most common bird of winter. Forms large foraging flocks. Found from river to Kaibab Plateau. In summer, nests among higher forests of ponderosa, spruce, and fir.
Remarks. Three subspecies found around canyon during year. Gray-headed junco breeds in canyon region during summer; in winter, it is joined by the Oregon junco, which has black head and upper body, and slate-colored junco, which is nearly all gray.

Blackbirds and Orioles

Most of these species are gregarious. Orioles tend to be colorful, while most blackbirds are black or dark. Twelve species found in park; eight are discussed.

RED-WINGED BLACKBIRD
(Agelaius phoeniceus)

Description. Length to nine inches. Black overall, with red shoulder bordered by yellow stripe.
Distribution. Marsh habitat. Sometimes found in very lower end of canyon near Lake Mead, where cattails and flooded vegetation provide nesting habitat.
Remarks. Male stakes out territory in reeds and defends it.

WESTERN MEADOWLARK
(Sturnella neglecta)

Description. Length to nine inches. Tan, streaked head and back, bright yellow underparts, bold black V-shaped patch on chest. Spotted sides.
Distribution. Open country of grasslands and sagebrush. Common in summer in House Rock Valley, Toroweap, South Rim, and elsewhere.
Remarks. Song is flutelike, bubbling sound, a sure harbinger of spring.

BREWER'S BLACKBIRD
(Euphagus cyanocephalus)

Description. Length to nine inches. Dark, glossy, metallic purple-green, yellow eye.
Distribution. Prefers open habitat. Found at the edge of meadows among aspen and near wet meadows on Kaibab Plateau. Occasionally found on South Rim.
Remarks. Often nests in colonies of several to 100 pairs.

GREAT-TAILED GRACKLE
(Quiscalus mexicanus)

Description. Length to eighteen inches. Large; male has purple cast to dark body with long black tail. Female brown with smaller tail.
Distribution. Open country with wetlands. Common along river corridor.
Remarks. Recently expanding range includes canyon. First one sighted in 1974.

BROWN-HEADED COWBIRD
(Molothrus ater)

Description. Length to seven inches. Male has brown head, purple-green body. Female has gray-brown back, pale underside.
Distribution. Common summer resident on rims and river.
Remarks. Does not build nest. Lays eggs in others birds' nests. Host is often fooled into raising cowbird as its own, often at expense of own offspring. Parasitism has devastated populations of some songbirds. Cowbirds have spread into many regions where they were previously rare, following domestic animals, including burros and horses.

HOODED ORIOLE
(Icterus cucullatus)

Description. Length to eight inches. Black back, tail, throat, face. Rest of bird bright orange. Two white wing bars.
Distribution. Riparian habitat. Common in summer along river and perennial tributaries like Havasu Creek.
Remarks. Has recently invaded canyon region; first sighted in 1974. Began breeding in area shortly thereafter.

BULLOCK'S ORIOLE
(*Icterus galbula*)

Description. Length to nine inches. Black crown, nape, throat, back, tail, wings. Orange over rest of body, including outer tail feathers. White shoulder patch on wing.
Distribution. Riparian-nesting bird. Common in summer in upper canyon near Lees Ferry.
Remarks. For two decades, the Bullock's and Baltimore orioles were considered to be a single species, called the northern oriole. New data, however, led taxonomists to officially reclassify the birds as two separate species in 1995.

SCOTT'S ORIOLE
(*Icterus parisorum*)

Description. Length to nine inches. Male has black head, shoulders, throat, tail, wings. Remainder is yellow, with yellow-white wing bars. Female lacks black and is generally greenish yellow.
Distribution. Prefers arid habitats. Summer resident of Joshua trees and yuccas on western fringe of canyon near Lake Mead. Occasionally seen in pinyon-juniper woodlands.
Remarks. One of the first species to head south for winter, leaving area in August.

Finches and Allies

These seedeaters often have thick bills. Form flocks. Ten species are found in the park; three are discussed.

CASSIN'S FINCH
(Carpodacus cassinii)

Description. Length to six inches. Red cap on male, streaked brown back and rosy breast, pale white belly. Female has streaked brown underparts, brown back.
Distribution. Prefers mountain forests. Common in summer on Kaibab Plateau and South Rim. Winters in pinyon-juniper woodlands just below rims.
Remarks. Sometimes forms breeding colonies. Flocks after breeding season.

PINE SISKIN
(Carduelis pinus)

Description. Length to five inches. Streaked brown with yellow wing bars and yellow near tail.
Distribution. Common in summer among forests on Kaibab Plateau and South Rim. During spring and fall, may be found inside canyon at mid-elevations such as Indian Gardens.
Remarks. Often forms flocks.

LESSER GOLDFINCH
(Carduelis psaltria)

Description. Length to 4.5 inches. Males have black crown, greenish back, yellow underparts. White wing bars.
Distribution. Common along woodland borders. Found in summer among riparian vegetation along river corridor as well as forested areas on rims.
Remarks. Gregarious; forms winter flocks of several hundred birds.

Old World Sparrows

This sparrowlike bird was introduced from Europe and always is associated with humans. One species is found in the park.

HOUSE SPARROW
(Passer domesticus)

Description. Length to six inches. Male has grayish crown, black throat and bib, brown back, tan belly. White cheek patch and wing bar. Female has brown back, lighter belly.
Distribution. Only around human habitation.
Remarks. A European species introduced into New York in mid-1800s. First found in Grand Canyon in 1919.

Mammals

Ecology and Description

Most mammals are four-legged creatures covered with hair or fur that bear live offspring and suckle the young. Unlike fish and reptiles, they maintain a constant body temperature. This feature allows mammals to live in many environments that are inhospitable to other animals, such as snowy uplands, where reptiles, amphibians, and other cold-blooded creatures would die.

Though mammals can survive in cold environments, cold is not the only factor they must cope with. For mammals living at higher elevations in the park, snow and seasonal shortages of food also are problems. Some, like small rodents, can survive under the insulating cover of snow. Other species move. Most bats fly south to milder climates, and mule deer move to lower elevations and south-facing slopes with milder temperatures and less snow. Some animals hibernate; chipmunks sleep away the winter in burrows, living off of stored fat.

A seasonally hot, dry place like the Grand Canyon places tremendous constraints upon many mammals. However, their warm-bloodedess allows them to remain active at night, when it is cooler. Nocturnal behavior is one reason why most mammals are seldom seen. Many species have excellent senses of smell, sight, and hearing, which allow for night foraging.

Another adaptation to coping with heat is behavioral. Many desert mammals retreat to burrows or shady cliffs during the day. Some sleep away periods of hot or cold temperatures. The golden-mantled ground squirrel retreats to its burrows and sleeps away the hottest summer months.

Water is another major concern for Grand Canyon mammals. Some get around this by never straying far from water. Mule deer and bighorn sheep make daily journeys to watering sources. Other species, such as the grasshopper mouse, obtain all the water they require from food. The kangaroo rat produces water metabolically by breaking down its food into water molecules. Also, it seldom urinates and plugs the entrance to its burrow to trap humidity. By remaining underground during the hottest time of the day, the kangaroo rat also reduces body temperatures and evaporative water loss.

Mammal Distribution

There are eighty-eight mammal species thought to live in the Grand Canyon region, though a few are so rare they are not discussed below. The region is defined as the entire park and some territory beyond, such as the river corridor from Lees Ferry to Lake Mead, plus the rims and plateaus of adjacent Indian reservations and other federal lands.

Several things affect the Grand Canyon's mammal distribution, diversity, and abundance. The elevation difference between the river and the highest parts of the Kaibab Plateau contributes to a mosaic of habitats. While wildlife is diverse, abundance is limited by the aridity and terrain. Deserts are not productive for life and, overall, the Grand Canyon doesn't support great numbers of most species. In addition, the steep terrain and plentiful cliffs significantly reduce the usable area for many land-based species.

Many mammals have needs that can be fulfilled only by certain terrain, vegetation, and climate. The following is a generalized list of mammal-habitat relationships. Some species are restricted to one or the other side of the river and are not necessarily found in all areas with the same habitat. For instance, the Uinta chipmunk is associated with the ponderosa forest but is found only on the North Rim.

The most restricted vegetative zone is the riparian—the greenbelt along watercourses of the Colorado River and its tributaries. Plants include the cottonwood, willow, desert willow, and the non-native tamarisk. Next to the riparian community within the Inner Gorge is the desert shrub zone, which includes catclaw, mesquite, saltbush, and some grasses. Mammal species found there include the spotted skunk, raccoon, beaver, Yuma myotis, ringtail, and rock pocket mouse.

Above the Inner Gorge at about 4,500 feet in the eastern and central portions of the canyon is the broad platform of the Tonto Plateau. This follows both sides of the river and is often a mile wide or more. The dominant plant of this section of the canyon is blackbrush. Other common plants are wolfberry, bursage, agave, narrowleaf yucca, burrobrush, and desert thorn. Mammals associated with this habitat includes the cliff chipmunk, white-tailed antelope squirrel, canyon mouse, cactus mouse, desert wood rat, white-throated wood rat, Ord's kangaroo rat, desert shrew, silky pocket mouse, ringtail, spotted skunk, rock squirrel, spotted ground squirrel, black-tailed jackrabbit, grasshopper mouse, and bighorn sheep.

The next major plant community is the pinyon-juniper woodland. It is found on the upper cliffs on both sides of the river as well as the South Rim. Plants include Utah juniper, pinyon pine, cliffrose, broadleaf yucca, serviceberry, rabbitbrush, ephedra, and blue grama. Mammals living in these woodlands include mule deer, mountain lion, gray fox, bobcat, rock squirrel, cliff chipmunk, Stephens wood rat, and pinyon mouse.

Lying between 7,000 and 7,400 feet on the South Rim and slightly higher on the North Rim is the ponderosa pine forest. Typical plants are the ponderosa, Gambel oak, locust, mountain mahogany, blue elderberry, creeping mahonia, and various fescue grasses. Mammals include the Abert squirrel on the South Rim, Kaibab squirrel on the North Rim, Uinta chipmunk, golden-mantled ground squirrel, Mexican wood rat, bushy-tailed wood rat, Mexican vole, porcupine, mountain cottontail, bobcat, mule deer, mountain lion, Merriam shrew, and striped skunk.

The highest-elevation plant community is found only on the North Rim. This includes the spruce-fir forest. Associated trees include aspen, white fir, Engelmann spruce, Douglas fir, and mountain ash. Mammals found in this zone include the red squirrel, northern pocket gopher, dwarf shrew, long-eared myotis, long-tailed vole, porcupine, mule deer, and Uinta chipmunk.

The Grand Canyon and Colorado River constitute a major physical barrier for many species. The canyon has only existed at its present depth for the past 2 million years or so, but during this period, there were major glaciations with cooling and warming periods that expanded and restricted some plant and animal populations. Eleven mammal species are restricted to the north side of the river, partly because habitat like spruce-fir forest is only located there. The red squirrel, a spruce-fir forest resident, is found only on the Kaibab Plateau within the park because that is the only portion of the park with such habitat. Fourteen other species are restricted to the south side of the river.

The following list after Hoffmeister (*Mammals of Grand Canyon*, 1971) shows the effect of the canyon on species distribution.

Species found primarily north of the river are the long-tailed vole, long-tailed pocket mouse, bushy-tailed wood rat, northern pocket gopher, red squirrel, Kaibab squirrel, least chipmunk, Uinta chipmunk, dwarf shrew, mountain cottontail, and golden-mantled ground squirrel.

Species found only south of the river include the Abert squirrel, Gunnison's prairie dog, silky pocket mouse, rock pocket mouse, Stephens wood rat, white-throated wood rat, Mexican wood rat, Mexican vole, and spotted ground squirrel.

Species restricted to the canyon itself are primarily desert dwellers or those with strong dependency upon the Colorado River water. They include the river otter, beaver, raccoon, bighorn sheep, desert wood rat, cactus mouse, canyon mouse, ringtail, spotted skunk, white-tailed antelope squirrel, rock pocket mouse, and long-tailed pocket mouse.

The Kaibab Deer Herd Story

One of the most famous wildlife stories in the United States is centered on the Kaibab Plateau. For decades, every college wildlife biology and ecology student has heard it. It is important and worth discussing here.

The Kaibab deer parable concludes that predators maintain prey species in balance with their food. According to the story, predators were systematically killed off on the plateau, the deer were free from predation, and the herd exploded. The large numbers of deer stripped their habitat, then starved in large numbers. The general lesson is that killing off predators is as bad for the prey as it is the predators.

Few dispute this general conclusion, but now there is some debate over the traditional interpretation of what happened to the Kaibab deer. The factors that control any animal population are complex, and though the destruction of predators may have contributed to changes in the deer herd, other events may also have been involved.

The Kaibab Plateau is an isolated forested upland that reaches more than 9,000 feet in elevation. It is managed as part of the North Rim of Grand Canyon National Park as well as the Kaibab National Forest. The events leading to the deer herd story may have been set in motion long before the 1920s, when the deer population is said to have exploded.

Much of this plateau was seriously overgrazed by domestic livestock.

More than 200,000 sheep, 20,000 cattle, and 3,000 horses were being grazed on the plateau well into the late 1890s. Indeed, at that time, there were far more domestic animals than deer grazing the Kaibab. Cattle and sheep prefer different plants than deer, though there is some overlap. Nevertheless, heavy grazing by domestic animals usually favors the growth of food (browse) plants preferred by deer. Livestock use of the plateau may have created changes in vegetation that temporarily favored expansion of deer herds.

In 1906, President Theodore Roosevelt set aside most of the plateau as a game reserve and hunting was banned. Until that time, market and subsistence hunting took a significant toll on deer in the region. With the declaration of the Kaibab as a game reserve, the human factor was largely removed.

At the time, it was deemed desirable to eradicate predators from the West, not only to benefit game animals but also to make rangelands safer for livestock. Government policy was to track down and eliminate all predators. Between 1906 and 1924, government hunters killed 3,024 coy-

Mountain lion and deer carcass. Mountain lions were once persecuted and hundreds were killed within the park. Their ecological value as a top predator is appreciated today, and they are now protected within the park.

otes, 674 mountain lions, and 21 wolves on the Kaibab. Ranchers continued to kill predators on adjacent lands.

With no hunting and no predators, deer flourished on the plateau. What happened next is subject to some debate. According to the traditional view, the deer herd grew from an estimated low of 4,000 in 1906 to 100,000 by 1924. Food supplies were stretched. Shrubs, the deer's preferred food, were heavily browsed.

Almost no rain fell during the summer of 1924. Since forage growth is almost directly tied to precipitation, this meant there was little new food. Deer went into the winter of 1924–25 in poor condition and many succumbed to starvation and stress. During the winter of 1924–25, three-quarters of the previous year's fawns died. Both adults and fawns continued to die in the following years so that by 1930, only an estimated 10,000 deer remained. The range was heavily browsed, with most of the lower branches bare of foliage.

As the deer began to die off, rescue efforts were attempted. One idea was to move the deer off the Kaibab Plateau by the Nankoweap Trail, across the river, and up the Tanner Trail to the South Rim. A group of 125 men was organized. Armed with tin cans and other noisemakers, they moved forward in a line. Gradually the human column became less organized. Deer slipped through the growing gaps between the marchers. By the time the men reached the Nankoweap Trailhead, there were, according to one observer, no deer in front of them and thousands behind. The deer continued to die.

The Kaibab deer herd crash is cited repeatedly as an example of how harmful a predator-prey imbalance can be. There is truth in the general idea, but new research has called into question many of the details and conclusions.

While many ecologists believe that predators can hold prey populations in check, in most of the nontropical zones, weather conditions, major fires, and other unpredictable natural events probably play at least as important a role in influencing animal herds. Predators alone ultimately cannot maintain a "balance," as has often been asserted.

Some evidence for this comes from the Kaibab deer herd itself. By the 1930s, the all-out war on predators in the region was halted. Mountain lions and coyotes were still being trapped, but there was no further attempt to eradicate them. Despite the growing number of predators, by 1945 deer herds had grown significantly and were estimated at 21,000 animals.

Game managers actually began to believe that a repeat of the 1920s crash was in the making. They wanted to stem the growth of the herd. In 1945, 1,000 permits were issued to hunt deer on the plateau. The number of permits continued to grow. More hunters took to the field, yet the herd was estimated at 57,000 in 1949. By 1954, more than 12,000 hunting permits were issued. Even this increasing human and natural predation could not stem the herd's growth. It all came tumbling down, not because of predation, but because of another severe winter in 1954–1955. The toll was put at 18,000 by spring.

More recently, among the few long-term studies that exist, similar findings have been made. A moose-wolf study on Isle Royale in Lake Michigan, for example, has shown that over a forty-year period, moose populations rose at the same time that wolf numbers grew. Even with predation, moose numbers continued to climb until a number of factors, including declining food quality, led to a crash. Despite the wolves, the moose population crashed. With little to eat, the number of wolves eventually declined as well. The decline in moose numbers has benefited its preferred foods, allowing for better nutrition. Recently, the moose population has begun to climb again, as have wolf numbers. Yet in other studies, such as among sea otters, which prey upon sea urchins, significant outside control of the amount of prey was found. All this shows that predator-prey relationships are not as tidy as previously thought.

This and other evidence has prompted some scientists to offer a different interpretation of the Kaibab deer herd story. One of the most immediate problems concerns deer numbers. All of these estimates are nothing more than informed guesses. At the time of the supposed crash of the deer herd in 1924–25, there were few observers and widely divergent estimates of deer numbers. Even today, estimates of game numbers, particularly in forested areas like the Kaibab, are nothing more than good guesses. Most wildlife agencies do not have the time or resources to conduct accurate counts. At best, such estimates are indicators of trends, not absolute numbers.

As early as 1969, Graeme Caughley, a New Zealand biologist, began to challenge the assumptions about the Kaibab herd. He wrote, "Little can be gleaned from the original records beyond the suggestion that the population began a decline sometime in the period 1924–1930, and that this decline was probably preceded by a period of increase. Any further conclusion is speculative."

The common assumption is that herbivores like deer should remain in some kind of balance with their food. That is an underlying assumption of range management and manipulation of grasslands for livestock. But some biologists suggest that this is an "economic" model, not an ecological one. If a predictable number of cattle or other animals is desirable year after year, ranchers do not stock the landscape with so many that none gain weight or that they die from starvation. Since cattle and other livestock do not tend to starve or die from disease or predators, they can have serious effects on a landscape over time.

The effect of livestock is seldom considered in the Kaibab story, but according to William Wright in his 1930s book, *Fauna of the National Parks of the United States*, "overstocking the range with domestic stock" contributed to the Kaibab "disaster" as well. The changes in vegetation wrought by heavy livestock grazing may have temporarily favored the growth of deer foods. That could have contributed to higher deer numbers until overbrowsing became a problem.

The livestock grazing may have also affected wildfire. The plant growth that helps sustain and carry fires is consumed by livestock. A loss of fire may have slowed the growth of new shrubs favored by deer. The timing of these events, one more immediate and the other delayed, may have prompted changes in the deer herd. As more and more deer consumed browse, the lack of fires may have led to a reduction in new shrub growth, which, along with drought and other factors, could have worsened conditions for herd growth.

If there was an "eruption" of deer at all, human factors may or may not have been responsible. That does not mean that some kind of equilibrium will not eventually return. Native species—predators, herbivores, and plants—evolve together over time. They continually change in number and distribution in response to pressures applied by one another. If the deer population rises, good forage becomes scarcer. Life becomes more difficult for the expanding herd. Under natural conditions, there are factors that often keep animal numbers in some kind of long-term balance. But this should not imply that populations of deer or any other animal or plant group should remain the same over time.

In many natural ecosystems, there are dramatic changes due to entirely unpredictable events. A wildfire may burn tens of thousands of acres, as in Yellowstone National Park in 1988. The fires dramatically altered the age and characteristics of the forest in that region, but it did not destroy the ecosystem. A deer herd may decline suddenly during a prolonged drought or after a severe winter, but it is seldom wiped out. When viewed from any short period of time, natural events are often characterized as catastrophic or a disaster. That is certainly how the Yellowstone fires were described by many journalists. Yet looking back at fire history, not only for the last ten or twenty years, but over centuries, scientists find that large fires, such as the one in 1988, are completely normal.

Some ecologists are now beginning to think that many wildlife populations also experience dramatic swings due to predators, weather, disease, and competition with other species. The importance of any one factor may vary, depending upon what happened in the past and current conditions. What is important is the temporal and geographical scale used to measure these changes. Just as a temperature of forty below one night of the year does not mean that we are entering another ice age, the decline or increase in a deer herd does not signal that anything is necessarily out of whack.

If there is a lesson in the Kaibab deer herd story, it is this: Do not tinker with nature. The introduction of livestock into the arid West was, and is, a big ecological mistake. Also, attacking predators is misguided. They are necessary, just as is wildfire. And looking at any natural event without perspective can be misleading. Despite the dire predictions, if we go back to the Kaibab Plateau today, we still find deer, mountain lions, and deer habitat.

Other Wildlife Issues

The Grand Canyon, like most of the West, has suffered the loss of some species, primarily because of human influences. Around the park, no other factor has had as great an effect on wildlife numbers as livestock production.

The most obvious human influence has been systematic slaughter of predators. At first, this was done randomly by ranchers. But predators came to symbolize "wild nature" to livestock operators, and they began an almost maniacal campaign to rid the West of all predators. With their strong political connections (even today, there are far more ranchers among western politicians than their small numbers would suggest), ranchers enlisted the federal government in their war on nature.

After 1915, it became federal policy to seek out and kill wolves, bears, mountain lions, and other large predators, as well as destroy grass-eating rodents like the prairie dog, which ranchers believed competed with their livestock for forage. The unfortunate situation is that ranchers still control much of the West and there still is predator and "pest" control, even within some national parks.

The net effect has been the loss of a number of species that formerly lived in or near the Grand Canyon. Though there is no grazing in the park today except for Indian animals, livestock production outside of the park still affects it. Predator control outside the park still influences wildlife distribution and interactions of predators within the park, since animals do not observe political boundaries.

The grizzly bear was probably the earliest casualty of the livestock industry in the region. In the arid Southwest, the grizzly was never abundant. It was restricted primarily to higher mountain areas and the riparian zones along major rivers. Grizzlies were common in the San Francisco Peaks and Bill Williams Mountains south of the canyon. Biologist Vernon Bailey reported them in the Pine Mountains near St. George, Utah. He also noted that a grizzly was killed on the Kaibab Plateau in the 1860s or 1870s. Today, the closest documented occurrence of grizzlies is in the Yellowstone National Park area of Wyoming. Bears were destroyed elsewhere as threats to livestock.

Another loser in the war on wildlife was the wolf. To appease the livestock industry, wolves were systematically hunted down, poisoned, trapped, and shot throughout the West, including the Grand Canyon region. According to Bailey, wolves were found on both rims. Between 1906 and 1924, a minimum of twenty-one wolves were reported killed on the Kaibab Plateau. Wolves are now extinct south of Yellowstone. With wolf restoration efforts in other parts of the West, it may be time to consider reintroduction of wolves to the Kaibab Plateau and other locations in the Southwest.

The jaguar, a large, heavily spotted cat, reached its northern range limits in the Grand Canyon region. A jaguar was killed just south of the park border in 1907 or 1908. It had killed a colt and was subsequently tracked down and destroyed. Jaguars were never common in Arizona, although as late as the 1970s a few were reported in southeastern Arizona. Like the wolf, the jaguar has always been persecuted by livestock interests.

Another species hurt by the livestock industry's war on wildlife is the prairie dog. They were once the most abundant mammal in North America, existing in the billions. Their population has declined to 2 percent of its former abundance. Now prairie dogs are so rare that three of the five species in North America are listed as endangered, and even the most abundant, the black-tailed prairie dog, was recently petitioned for listing as threatened. The species found in the park, Gunnison's prairie dog, is endangered.

Prairie dogs form colonies, making them easy to locate and eradicate. The usual method is to spread poisoned grain about the colony. Animals die a painful death. A small colony of Gunnison's prairie dogs lived for decades in Pasture Wash near the park border east of Havasu Canyon. According to Hoffmeister, they were abundant in this area in 1942 and 1946, but in 1948, only fifteen were seen. In 1959, another eight to ten prairie dogs were reported in this area. They have been poisoned a number of times and it is unclear whether any remain today.

The reduction in prairie dogs has had serious consequences for many other species. The black-footed ferret, a predator of prairie dogs, once ranged into northeast Arizona. Because of the dramatic decline of prairie dogs throughout the West, the ferret itself is now endangered and the rarest mammal in North America. Other prairie dog–associated species that are no longer found in the park include the burrowing owl, which lives in prairie dog burrows and feeds on them.

Yet another animal that has suffered from livestock production is the swift pronghorn antelope. Antelope were not native to the canyon (though there once was a small introduced herd), but they were common on the pinyon-juniper grasslands south of the canyon and below the Vermillion Cliffs east of the Kaibab Plateau. Antelope are still found in the House-rock Valley region. Pronghorns were occasionally found along the South Rim, though not in recent years.

Overhunting in the last century had as much to do with the decline of the antelope as anything, but more recently they have been hindered by domestic livestock on most of the public lands outside of national parks. Livestock compete with antelope for forage, particularly for the scarce patches of green in summer. Antelope enter winter in poorer condition and bear smaller, weaker fawns that are vulnerable to predators and spring storms.

There was an attempt earlier in this century to establish an antelope herd within the canyon—ironically, in a location where they never had been found before. In 1924, eleven were released onto the Tonto Plateau near Indian Gardens. By 1944, the herd had grown slowly to as many as thirty, but the plateau had limited forage and was poor habitat for antelope. Eventually, this herd died out.

The bighorn sheep has also been harmed by the introduction of domestic animals into the West. Wild sheep are susceptible to diseases carried by livestock. Also, in areas heavily grazed by domestic animals, forage needed by wild bighorns can be drastically reduced, leading to starvation or increasing susceptibility to disease.

Bighorn sheep were once common in rugged terrain like the Grand Canyon. Indian stories indicated that bighorns were once numerous in the canyon. Even after the turn of the century, records show estimates of more than 500 wild sheep inhabiting the park. But there have been big die-offs due to disease. Even though livestock do not inhabit the park (except for the Indian animals), wild sheep, particularly rams, wander widely and occasionally come into contact with domestic animals. Periodic die-offs due to disease will remain a threat to the park's wild sheep. As long as livestock are grazed on lands around the park, bighorns will probably never fully recover to their former abundance.

Species Accounts

Shrews

Shrews are the smallest and rarest mammals in Grand Canyon National Park. They look like small mice with pointed snouts, small ears, and velvety fur. Most are less than four inches long. If you have the chance to examine one closely, you can tell a shrew from a mouse by the five toes on its front feet. A mouse has only four, although I would not recommend handling a live shrew.

Shrews forage on the ground and under vegetation, seldom venturing from cover. Shrew eyes are very small. The animals rely primarily upon smell and hearing to detect prey. Like bats, shrews make ultrahigh twittering squeaks to assist in navigation.

Because of their small body size and the high loss of heat to the environment, shrews must consume a tremendous amount of high-protein food to maintain their internal temperature. If they are deprived of food for even a few hours, they can die from "exposure." Their high-protein diet means shrews are primarily insectivores, but they also eat other invertebrates like earthworms. They can produce a mild poison to subdue prey.

MERRIAM SHREW
(Sorex merriami)

Description. Small eyes and ears. Body 3.5 to 4 inches. Brownish gray above, white or pale underparts, including tail.
Distribution. Relatively rare. Found primarily at higher elevations in moist coniferous forests, typically associated with grassy meadows.
Remarks. Although numbers are sparse in any location, this is the most widely distributed shrew in the West. Named for C. Hart Merriam, first chief of the U.S. Biological Survey. Builds ball-like nest in grass. Nocturnal.

DESERT SHREW
(Notiosorex crawfordi)

Description. Grayish, short tail, large ears. Body 3.2 to 3.5 inches. Tail less than half the length of body (in other shrews, tails are longer).
Distribution. Very rare. Associated with desert areas. Found below pinyon pine–juniper zone, primarily with sagebrush, blackbrush, and other aridlands vegetation.
Remarks. Like other desert mammals, can obtain water from eating prey. Builds small, round, birdlike nests beneath rocks and larger plants. Has been found along Bright Angel and Hermit trails, as well as north of the Colorado in Zion and the Arizona Strip.

DWARF SHREW
(Sorex nanus)

Description. Long tail (1.5 inches) compared with other shrews. Overall length four inches. Grayish with brown; underparts grayish, but lighter than above.
Distribution. Spruce-fir forests on Kaibab Plateau.
Remarks. One of the smallest shrews. Always associated with subalpine-alpine habitats, as far north as Montana.

Bats

This is the second most common mammal group in the world. Bats look like flying mice, except for their barrel-shaped chests with their large muscles.

Bats are the only mammals that truly fly. Their wings are formed by skin membrane stretched across what would be finger bones. Bats have taken over the nighttime niche of insect-eating birds. They navigate in the dark by use of echolocation, which functions similarly to radar.

Most bats produce only one pup per year. Since the males do not rear the young, the baby must accompany the female on her nightly feeding forays. Because of their small body size and large skin surface area, bats lose heat easily. In winter, bats cluster to conserve heat. They also drop their body temperature to match closely surrounding air, reducing heat loss.

YUMA MYOTIS
(Myotis yumanensis)

Description. Medium-sized bat with pale ears. Color is dull, pale brown. Body is 3.2 to 3.5 inches. Hairy wing membrane is a distinctive feature.
Distribution. Near water, principally along Colorado River and tributaries.
Remarks. Fairly common. Roosts in cliffs by waterways. Comes out at night to capture insects, darting after prey just above water surface.

LONG-EARED MYOTIS
(Myotis evotis)

Description. Very large ears (up to one inch long). Back is brown, belly lighter. Body length 3.2 to 3.75 inches.
Distribution. Common on North Rim among spruce-fir forest, but feeds in grassy meadows and other forest openings.
Remarks. Often roosts in old buildings.

FRINGE-TAILED MYOTIS
(Myotis thysanodes)

Description. Large, brown bat with silvery underparts, long ears, large feet, fringe of hair on tail membrane. Length to four inches.
Distribution. Found on both rims but not in bottom of canyon.
Remarks. Primarily eats beetles. Hibernates in winter. Seldom seen. Does not usually appear until twilight has turned to darkness.

LONG-LEGGED MYOTIS
(Myotis volans)

Description. Chocolate fur; occasionally lighter. Keeled calcar (tarsal bone). Short, round, black ears. Short nose, steeply rising forehead. Body 3.7 to 4.5 inches.
Distribution. Coniferous forests on both rims. Most common bat in South Rim forest.
Remarks. Eats moths, other insects.

CALIFORNIA MYOTIS
(Myotis californicus)

Description. Smallest bat, 2.8 to 3.5 inches. Yellowish or rusty fur contrasts sharply with black ears.
Distribution. Most common bat in canyon bottom and side canyons, though found up to rims among pines.
Remarks. Lives in small colonies or alone. Has erratic flight pattern, dipping suddenly up and down for insects.

SMALL-FOOTED MYOTIS
(Myotis leibii)

Description. Small with chocolate back. Black ears. Body up to four inches.
Distribution. Uncommon. South Rim in eastern part of park.
Remarks. Not much is known about this bat.

SILVER-HAIRED BAT
(Lasionycteris noctivagans)

Description. Large, up to 4.2 inches. Black, some hairs frosted. Wings and short ears are black. Fur covers half of top portion of tail membrane.
Distribution. Rare. Reported in juniper-pinyon pine and ponderosa pine zone on South Rim.
Remarks. Solitary. Seems to roost under bark and inside large, hollow trees, thus dependent upon old-growth forest.

WESTERN PIPISTRELLE
(Pipistrellus hesperus)

Description. Smallest bat in Grand Canyon. Body 2.5 to 3.5 inches. Pale gray. Ears, wings, tail membrane black.
Distribution. Most common bat in Grand Canyon. Found along river and on both rims. Lives in cliff walls.
Remarks. Often begins flying in daylight. Often seen around Bright Angel Lodge and El Tovar complex. Adults weigh one-tenth to one-twentieth of an ounce. Despite size, one of few Grand Canyon bats to bear twins.

BIG BROWN BAT
(Eptesicus fuscus)

Description. Large; four to five inches. Color pale brown to chocolate. Underparts slightly lighter. Face, ears darker than rest.
Distribution. Most common large bat associated with coniferous forests on both rims.
Remarks. Size, color make identification easier. Only the light-colored hoary bat is larger. Can fly up to forty miles per hour, fastest of any bat. Like many bats, it hibernates. Body fat may account for up to a third of weight.

RED BAT
(Lasiurus borealis)

Description. Not always red. Males rusty to reddish brown; females yellowish tinted with red. Back hair sometimes frosted, particularly in females. Wing membranes black with fur on tail membrane. Body 3.5 to 4.2 inches.
Distribution. Relatively rare. Found in canyon bottoms with large trees, such as Bright Angel Creek near Phantom Ranch.
Remarks. *Lasiurus* means "shaggy tail" in Latin, a reference to furry tail membrane. Prefers to roost in trees, often mimicking a dead leaf.

HOARY BAT
(Lasiurus cinereus)

Description. Large. Body 4.5 to 5.5 inches. Frosted hair. Face, underside of wings yellowish. Ears small and round, rimmed in black. Distinctive cream-colored spot at base of narrow wings.
Distribution. Rare. Found only along canyon bottom. Probably a migrant.
Remarks. Largest bat in North America. Often roosts in trees.

TOWNSEND'S BIG-EARED BAT
(Plecotus townsendii)

Description. Large bat. Body 3.5 to 4.5 inches. Large, thin ears, nearly transparent. Lumps on either side of nose gave nickname "lump-nosed bat." Upper body tan, underside lighter.
Distribution. South Rim. Associated elsewhere with pinyon-juniper and ponderosa forests.
Remarks. Highly maneuverable. Can hover. Feeds primarily on moths.

PALLID BAT
(Antrozous pallidus)

Description. Large; 4.2 to 5.5 inches. Squarish face. Large ears, separate at base, differentiate it from Townsend's big-eared bat. Most distinguishing feature is yellowish brown color. Wartlike bumps on face.
Distribution. Desert species. Common along canyon bottoms and side canyons including Havasu Canyon and Indian Gardens area; occasionally seen near rims.
Remarks. Often hunts by walking. Favorite foods are scorpions, crickets, beetles. Will even prey on mice. Also eats fruit, seeds of cactus and agave.

MEXICAN FREE-TAILED BAT
(Tadarida brasiliensis)

Description. Smoky brown fur. Body 3.5 to 4.5 inches. Tail extends beyond tail membrane (hence the name "free-tailed"). Upper lip wrinkled.
Distribution. Uncommon. Found on both rims and canyon. Roosts in caves.
Remarks. This is one of the most abundant bats in North America. Swarms of this species at Carlsbad Caverns in New Mexico. Very fast, highly migratory.

Hares and Rabbits

Hares and rabbits look similar, but young hares are born fully furred and with eyes open, whereas rabbit young are naked and blind. Hares are also larger than rabbits and more likely to run than hide. Both hares and rabbits produce two kinds of feces: a hard one, like a small dark pellet, and a soft one that is reingested, a practice called coprophagy. Reingestion is probably done to extract additional nutrients from diet.

DESERT COTTONTAIL
(Sylvilagus auduboni)

Description. Medium size, body fourteen to sixteen inches. Grayish brown. Short, white tail.
Distribution. Arid portions of South Rim among sagebrush grasslands and pinyon-juniper forests.
Remarks. Most active at dawn and dusk. Can swim and climb trees; prefers burrows abandoned by badgers and other mammals.

MOUNTAIN COTTONTAIL
(Sylvilagus nuttallii)

Description. Similar to desert cottontail. Small, white, cottony tail. Slightly smaller. Body to fifteen inches. Black line on edge of ear.
Distribution. North Rim among sagebrush flats.
Remarks. Active at dawn and dusk. Sagebrush is favorite food.

BLACK-TAILED JACKRABBIT
(Lepus californicus)

Description. Large hare up to twenty-five inches in length with huge ears up to seven inches. Long hind legs. Gray body, top of tail and tips of ears black.
Distribution. Open country on both rims, typically sagebrush or cactus.
Remarks. Outruns predators. Speed up to forty miles per hour; leaps twenty feet or more. Rarely drinks, obtaining most of its water from food.

Squirrels, Chipmunks, and Prairie Dogs

GUNNISON'S PRAIRIE DOG
(Cynomys gunnisoni)

Description. Short-legged, short-tailed, ground-dwelling rodent. Body thirteen to fourteen inches. Cinnamon brown, white-tipped tail.
Distribution. South Rim. Arid grasslands.
Remarks. May be gone from park. Previously found at Pasture Wash on south edge of park. Rare throughout range due to poisoning programs and disease. Endangered.

SPOTTED GROUND SQUIRREL
(Spermophilus spilosoma)

Description. Small; seven to ten inches. Small white spots against reddish brown back and sides. Thinly furred, black-tipped tail.
Distribution. Open, arid terrain. Found on South Rim by Pasture Wash.
Remarks. Eats seeds, grass, lizards, grasshoppers, kangaroo rats. Unlike most rodents, is active by day. Hibernates in colder weather.

ROCK SQUIRREL
(Spermophilus variegatus)

Description. Large ground squirrel. Seventeen inches. Gray with white specks. Lower back sometimes reddish. Bushy tail similar to that of gray squirrel of eastern United States.

Distribution. Common in many canyon locales, including along river and on both rims.

Remarks. This is the ground squirrel most likely to be seen begging for food at rim viewpoints. Nests in rocks and among cliffs. Climbs trees for cones.

GOLDEN-MANTLED GROUND SQUIRREL
(Spermophilus lateralis)

Description. Looks like a big chipmunk, minus facial stripes. Sides have characteristic broad white stripe, bordered in black. Shoulders cinnamon red, hence the name "golden-mantled." Body nine to twelve inches.

Distribution. Moist woods and meadow edges. Common in the North Rim coniferous forests.

Remarks. Bold, active in daylight. Hibernates in winter. Cheek pouches used to take food back to den.

The golden-mantled ground squirrel looks like a giant chipmunk, but lacks stripes on its face.

WHITE-TAILED ANTELOPE SQUIRREL
(*Ammospermophilus leucurus*)

Description. Chipmunklike ground squirrel with white, unbordered stripe. Underside of tail flashy white. Tail held vertical when running. Body eight to nine inches.

Distribution. Found in arid, sparsely vegetated regions. Found on river, Tonto Plateau, South Rim, likely elsewhere.

Remarks. One of the few ground squirrels active in really hot weather. Does not sweat but can maintain normal body temperatures even as air exceeds 100 degrees. Like pronghorn antelope, this squirrel "flashes" its conspicuous white tail when running. Eats many fruits and seeds. Will climb juniper trees for berries.

LEAST CHIPMUNK
(*Eutamias minimus*)

Description. Small; seven to eight inches. Lightest of any western chipmunk. Has four white and five black narrow stripes on back and sides. Orange-brown sides, pale belly. Underside of tail yellowish.

Distribution. North Rim. Mostly open coniferous forests among grassy openings.

Remarks. Climbs trees.

UINTA CHIPMUNK
(*Eutamias umbrinus*)

Description. Large; 8 to 9.5 inches. Black-and-white stripe pattern like that of least chipmunk, but has faint or no lateral-most black stripe. White belly. Ears blackish in front and whitish behind.

Distribution. Tree dwellers. Found in North Rim coniferous forests.

Remarks. Most common chipmunk at North Rim campgrounds and scenic areas.

CLIFF CHIPMUNK
(Eutamias dorsalis)

Description. Only chipmunk in canyon with indistinct stripes. Stripes more obvious on head than on back. Tail rusty below and dark above. Body seven to nine inches.

Distribution. Only chipmunk on South Rim. Also found in canyon at Indian Gardens, Havasu Canyon, and to edge of North Rim.

Remarks. Gives sharp, rapid barks, each accompanied by a twitch of tail. Prefer cliffs and rocks, but found among pinyon-juniper woodlands.

ABERT SQUIRREL
(Sciurus aberti aberti)

Description. Large, bushy-eared tree squirrel. Back and sides gray, including top of tail. Underparts, including underside of tail, whitish. Ears have conspicuous tufts, sometimes absent in summer.

Distribution. Ponderosa pine forests. South Rim only.

Remarks. Primarily eats pine cone seeds and fungi. Does not hibernate. Active all winter and feeds on the inner bark of twigs from ponderosa pine.

KAIBAB SQUIRREL
(Sciurus aberti kaibabensis)

Description. North Rim counterpart to Abert squirrel. Gray with black or dark underside. Bushy tail is white.

Distribution. North Rim only. Endemic to Kaibab Plateau.

Remarks. The Kaibab squirrel was once thought to be a separate species; now considered a subspecies of Abert squirrel. Becoming rare outside of Grand Canyon National Park due to logging of old-growth pine forests, upon which it depends.

RED SQUIRREL
(*Tamiasciurus hudsonicus*)

Description. Tree squirrel, rusty gray with white underparts. Distinctive black band separates belly from back. Ears small. White eye ring. Length twelve to fourteen inches.
Distribution. North Rim coniferous forests.
Remarks. Often chatters loudly if agitated. Found in spruce-fir zone above ponderosa pine zone dominated by larger Kaibab squirrel. Active all winter; eats cones cached in previous autumn.

Pocket Gophers

These are burrowing rodents with large incisor teeth and long front claws for digging. They have tiny eyes and fur-lined cheek pouches. Gophers typically plug burrow openings, whereas ground squirrels do not.

COMMON POCKET GOPHER
(*Thomomys bottae*)

Description. Small ears, tiny eyes, large front teeth, well-clawed front feet. Short, hairless tail and huge cheek pouches. Rich brown color. Overall length 7 to 9.5 inches.
Distribution. South Rim and Kanab Creek area on north side of river.
Remarks. Burrows are seldom seen. Presence is often visible as dirt mounds snaking across ground.

NORTHERN POCKET GOPHER
(Thomomys talpoides)

Description. Similar to common pocket gopher, but with white patch below mouth and black patch behind ear.
Distribution. Meadows on North Rim.
Remarks. Like all pocket gophers, this is a vegetarian, eating mostly bulbs, roots, other tubers.

Pocket Mice and Kangaroo Rats

These are small- to medium-sized mice known for jumping. They have notably long hind legs and feet with longish tails. Pocket mice are more closely related to gophers than to true mice. One telling feature is the cheek pouches. The Latin genus name for pocket mice, *Perognathus*, means "pouch-jawed." Kangaroo rats have large, powerful hind legs and feet. They jump rather than scurry. When pursued, some kangaroo rats have been known to jump nine feet.

All pocket mice and kangaroo rats are nocturnal, so they can seem scarce. All burrow and are predominately seed gathers. Nearly all of the following species are adapted to arid living. Most can survive without drinking, relying upon efficient kidneys and moisture found in foods.

SILKY POCKET MOUSE
(Perognathus flavus)

Description. Small jumping mouse with large hind feet. Soft fur. White underside, buff above. Body up to 4.8 inches, with tail up to 2.3 inches. Yellow mark behind ear; frequently white spot below it.
Distribution. Sandy soils in arid locations including sagebrush, blackbrush, and pinyon-juniper habitats.
Remarks. Smallest rodent in park. Burrows and caches seeds for future consumption.

ROCK POCKET MOUSE
(Perognathus intermedius)

Description. Medium-sized yellowish gray jumping mouse. Overall length seven inches with up to four-inch tail. Bushy tail, bicolored gray above and white below, longer than body. Spinelike hairs protrude from rump.
Distribution. Prefers cliffs and rocky slopes, but also found in sandy sites with blackbrush. Found from Tonto Plateau and Inner Gorge south of the Colorado.
Remarks. Burrows provide good insulation from heat. Biologist Vernon Bailey found that the temperature one foot below ground's surface was 82 degrees Fahrenheit at 9 A.M. following a day when the ground-level temperature had been 144 degrees Fahrenheit.

LONG-TAILED POCKET MOUSE
(Perognathus formosus)

Description. Tail up to 4.8 inches. Overall length up to eight inches. Tail gray above, white below with crest of dark tufts over the last third. Large feet.
Distribution. North side of Colorado River at Nankoweap Canyon and Deer Creek Falls, among other sites. Found in sandy areas and among blackbrush and cacti.
Remarks. Not found in park until 1969.

ORD'S KANGAROO RAT
(Dipodomys ordii)

Description. Large jumping mouse (up to ten inches) with tail up to six inches. Upper body buffy yellow, underparts white. Hind feet white.
Distribution. Open desert with loose sandy soils. Mostly known from Pasture Wash area south of the canyon.
Remarks. Can leap up to nine feet.

MERRIAM KANGAROO RAT
(Dipodomys merriami)

Description. Smallest kangaroo rat. Light buff above, white below. Dark hip patch rimmed by white stripe. Total body length up to ten inches.
Distribution. Primarily along river at western end of canyon.
Remarks. Named for C. Hart Merriam, early mammalogist.

Beavers

Beavers are large rodents, weighing up to sixty pounds, that form colonies and live primarily in water.

BEAVER
(Castor canadensis)

Description. Large, dark brown rodent with flattened tail and webbed hind feet. Large teeth. Overall length up to forty-eight inches.
Distribution. Colorado River and tributaries.
Remarks. Watertight membranes cover eyes and keep water from entering ears and nostrils. Can remain submerged for up to fifteen minutes. Many Grand Canyon beavers live in bank burrows instead of lodges.

New World Mice and Rats

This group includes wood rats, voles, harvest mice, grasshopper mice, and the *Peromyscus* or white-footed mice. These rodents have large eyes and ears, tails about equal to the length of the body, and light underparts.

WESTERN HARVEST MOUSE
(*Reithrodontomys megalotis*)

Description. Large ears. Overall length five to six inches. Reddish brown above, whitish underneath, longish tail.
Distribution. Throughout park at all elevations.
Remarks. Primarily seedeaters. A new litter weighs more than 50 percent of female's body.

CANYON MOUSE
(*Peromyscus crinitus*)

Description. Yellowish brown, sometimes with black highlights fading to whitish below. Overall length is six to seven inches. Tail has terminal tuft and is 3 to 4.8 inches—longest of the *Peromyscus* in the park. Small ears, white feet.
Distribution. Among rocks and clefts in canyon walls at all elevations in non-forested sections of the canyon.
Remarks. Most brightly colored *Peromyscus* in Grand Canyon.

CACTUS MOUSE
(*Peromyscus eremicus*)

Description. Medium-sized; overall length 7.5 to 8.5 inches. Tail up to 4.5 inches. Tail lacks prominent tuft. White feet.
Distribution. Associated with blackbrush–greasewood–prickly pear habitat of Tonto Plateau in inner portion of canyon.
Remarks. Biologist Vernon Bailey reported species was abundant in canyon during 1930s.

DEER MOUSE
(*Peromyscus maniculatus*)

Description. Reddish brown fading to white underparts. Overall length six to seven inches. Tail 2.2 to 3.2 inches, shortest of the five *Peromyscus* species in park. Large eyes. Small ears rimmed in white. White feet.
Distribution. Throughout canyon at all elevations; most common on rims and at higher elevations.
Remarks. One of the most widespread mice in United States; only place it is not found is Southeast.

BRUSH MOUSE
(*Peromyscus boylei*)

Description. Upper parts brownish, lighter beneath. Overall length seven to eight inches. Tail longer than head and body. White feet.
Distribution. Widest distribution of any *Peromyscus* species in park. Found from forests of North Rim to juniper forest and cottonwood stands along Bright Angel Creek at bottom of canyon.
Remarks. Eats seeds and berries, occasionally insects.

PINYON MOUSE
(*Peromyscus truei*)

Description. Dark brown above, whitish below. Large ears up to an inch long. Overall length seven to eight inches. Tail shorter than head and body and is furry. White feet.
Distribution. Rocky areas with pinyon pine.
Remarks. Eats pinyon nuts. Most arboreal of tree-dwelling mice.

NORTHERN GRASSHOPPER MOUSE
(Onychomys leucogaster)

Description. Short-tailed mouse with brownish gray fur and white underparts. Coloration varies with age, more grayish in youth and old age. Overall length 5.5 to 6 inches. Tail 1.5 to 2 inches.
Distribution. South Rim.
Remarks. Eats crickets, scorpions, spiders, grasshoppers. Unlike most mice, males help rear young, bringing food to babies. Will make a shrill whistle while standing on hind legs.

WHITE-THROATED WOOD RAT
(Neotoma albigula)

Description. Large; 12.5 to 13.5 inches overall. Brownish gray above, whitish below. Long tail, 5.5 to 6.5 inches, hairy but not bushy. Throat white to base. White feet.
Distribution. Drier parts of canyon, primarily Tonto Plateau among blackbrush–greasewood–prickly pear cactus habitat. Also on more arid parts of South Rim.
Remarks. Known as pack rats, wood rats typically build nests up to four feet high using anything, including bones, twigs, paper, mule droppings.

DESERT WOOD RAT
(Neotoma lepida)

Description. Ten to twelve inches overall. Yellowish brown to gray above, lighter below. May have white patch on throat. White hind feet.
Distribution. Found in many habitats, but more common among cliffs and rocks of North Rim.
Remarks. Only wood rat in park to live on both sides of river.

STEPHENS WOOD RAT
(Neotoma stephensi)

Description. Similar in size to desert wood rat, but tail is hairy to bushy. Dusky wedged-shaped pattern on hind foot.
Distribution. South side of canyon. Rocky places near and among juniper-pinyon.
Remarks. Varied diet, but juniper foliage is favored.

MEXICAN WOOD RAT
(Neotoma mexicana)

Description. Overall length thirteen to fifteen inches. Looks like white-throated wood rat except throat hairs are grayish at base instead of white. Underparts grayish; brown spot on chest. Distinctly bicolored tail.
Distribution. Among rocky areas on South Rim. Pinyon pine and ponderosa forests.
Remarks. As name implies, species is more common south of the border. The Grand Canyon is northern fringe of range.

BUSHY-TAILED WOOD RAT
(Neotoma cinerea)

Description. Bushy, squirrel-like tails; large hind feet; overall length thirteen to seventeen inches. Musky scent used to mark territory.
Distribution. Among rocks on North Rim only.
Remarks. The animal known as a "pack rat." Hauls off anything it can find, including ribbons, bits of metal, twigs, cones, and small rocks.

LONG-TAILED VOLE
(Microtus longicaudus)

Description. Small mouselike creature, brownish above and grayish below. Overall length 6 to 7.5 inches. Tail one-third the length of body, long for a vole.
Distribution. Moist meadows on North Rim.
Remarks. Principal food is grass. Makes well-defined runways in grass. Takes to water readily.

American Porcupines

Porcupines are large rodents covered with long spines (quills) that are used in defense. Slow moving and seemingly dim-witted, porcupines feed primarily upon bark.

PORCUPINE
(Erethizon dorsatum)

Description. Overall length twenty-six to thirty-three inches. Sharp quills cover animal on all parts except belly. Short tail. Eyes small and beady; ears small.
Distribution. Forested areas on both rims.
Remarks. Common but seldom seen because of nocturnal habits. Quills protect against most enemies, but mountain lions can capture and eat porcupines.

Dog Family

Members of the dog family are carnivores with pointed ears, long legs, and long muzzles. Tails are often bushy and thick. Hind feet have only four claws.

The only fox found in the park is the gray fox, but it sometimes has a reddish cast, so it is occasionally confused with the red fox. No red foxes are found near the Grand Canyon, however.

Wolves were found on both rims at one time but were wiped out by the 1930s, as they were throughout the West, to appease livestock interests. Reportedly, the wolf found on the South Rim was the Mexican wolf. Recent efforts may lead to reintroduction or recolonization of this region.

Coyotes feed primarily on small rodents and rabbits. They are occasionally heard howling and yipping in the evening hours.

COYOTE
(Canis latrans)

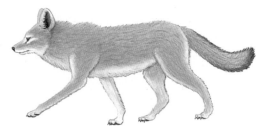

Description. Small to medium-sized doglike animal up to fifty inches long. Usually grayish to brown with buff-colored underparts. Long-legged, long-muzzled, with pointy ears.

Distribution. Throughout park, but more abundant at higher elevations than within Inner Gorge.

Remarks. Often howls and yips at night. Feeds primarily on rabbits, mice, small birds, carrion, occasionally deer, and almost anything else it can catch or find.

GRAY FOX
(Urocyon cinereoargenteus)

Description. Medium-sized fox thirty-six to forty-two inches overall. Pointed ears. Dark gray above with reddish brown flanks. Underparts whitish. Reddish brown, bushy tail with black stripe on top.

Distribution. Throughout park.

Remarks. Eats insects, small rodents, rabbits, and fruit, including that of prickly pear cactus. Dens in rock crevices, hollow logs, old badger dens. Good tree climber.

Bears

Bears are the largest land carnivores, with large heads, small ears, and smallish eyes. Though they love meat, they are primarily vegetarians, consuming a wide variety of roots, berries, and grass. All bears in the Grand Canyon area are black bears, although grizzly bears once roamed in southwestern Utah's Pine Mountains and in the San Francisco Peaks to the south of the canyon.

BLACK BEAR
(*Ursus americanus*)

Description. Brown or black. Up to five feet in overall length, two to three feet tall. Short tail. Claws on front paws no more than two inches long.
Distribution. Rare. Found in forests on both rims, though not in recent years.
Remarks. Mostly nocturnal. Vegetation is its primary food, so most of the Grand Canyon is poor habitat because of its aridity.

Raccoon Family

Two raccoons are found in the Grand Canyon, the raccoon and the ringtail. Both are medium-sized carnivores with ringed tails. Both are good climbers.

RACCOON
(*Procyon lotor*)

Description. Small masked animal with a striped tail. Fur is grayish. Walk is flat-footed. Body thirty-three to thirty-six inches long.
Distribution. Waterways, primarily along Colorado River or lower ends of tributaries.
Remarks. Eats cactus fruit, small birds, eggs, fish.

RINGTAIL
(*Bassariscus astutus*)

Description. Size of house cat. Grayish brown. Overall length twenty-five to thirty inches. Thinner than raccoon, with longer striped black-and-white tail.
Distribution. Most of the canyon except for highest parts of North Rim. Primarily associated with rocky cliff areas.
Remarks. Sometimes called "ringtail cat" for its resemblance to domestic cat. One of the most common carnivores in the canyon, but seldom seen because of its nocturnal habits.

Weasel Family

This group includes weasels, skunks, badgers, and river otters. All have scent glands, though they are best developed in skunks. These animals typically have sharp teeth, short legs, and long tails.

LONG-TAILED WEASEL
(Mustela frenata)

Description. Long, lean, with long, black-tipped tail and short legs. Generally brown, though turns white in winter. Underparts orangish with white chin.
Distribution. Wooded areas at higher elevations on both rims. More common on North Rim.
Remarks. Eats mostly mice and voles. Will hunt under snow.

The badger is a member of the weasel family. It uses its sharp claws to dig out the burrows of ground squirrels and other burrowing rodents.

AMERICAN BADGER
(*Taxidea taxus*)

Description. Squat, short-legged; short, bushy tail. White stripe from tip of nose over head and down back. Brownish gray on top, underparts yellowish-white. Overall length twenty-three to thirty-one inches.

Distribution. Both rims.

Remarks. Hunts ground squirrels, prairie dogs, mice, and other burrowing animals. Exceptional diggers; will excavate burrows to capture prey.

WESTERN SPOTTED SKUNK
(*Spilogale putorius*)

Description. Small black-and-white animal with bushy tail. Tip of tail is white. White spot between eyes; white spots on back and sides.

Distribution. Along Colorado River and Inner Gorge below 4,500 feet.

Remarks. Common in canyon. Found in rocks and caves but never far from water. Eats small birds, eggs, insects, mice. Often heard foraging through dried leaves at night. Best known for its strong scent, used as a defense.

STRIPED SKUNK
(*Mephitis mephitis*)

Description. Slightly larger than house cat; up to twenty-seven inches in length overall. Bushy tail. White stripe runs from tip of nose to tip of tail, splitting into two stripes along back.

Distribution. Forests on South Rim and perhaps North Rim.

Remarks. Strong scent glands. Distinctive odor used to discourage predators. During colder winters, will den up and become dormant, but does not hibernate.

RIVER OTTER
(Lutra canadensis)

Description. Dark brown, short-legged, thick-tailed, and weasel-like. Larger than house cat; up to fifty inches long. Webbed feet. Tapered tail .

Distribution. Colorado River. Very rare, seldom reported in park.

Remarks. Eats fish and shellfish. Exceptional swimmer.

Cat Family

The cats are among the most carnivorous land animals. There are two representatives in the canyon: the mountain lion and bobcat. Both have retractable claws.

MOUNTAIN LION
(Felis concolor)

Description. Long-tailed, large, uniformly tawny. Sometimes mistaken for large dog or deer. Overall length up to eight feet, with tail two to three feet in length. Large paws. A large lion will weigh up to 275 pounds.

Distribution. Throughout park.

Remarks. Also known as cougar, puma, panther, and catamount. Feeds primarily on deer; will take elk. One of the few animals that can prey upon porcupine. Stalks and pounces instead of running down game like a wolf. In the past, mountain lions were persecuted as predators. One hunter in 1909 killed eighty lions in one season. Uncle Jim Owen, over the course of many years, killed more than 600 mountain lions in the Grand Canyon and Kaibab Plateau. Now protected in park.

Bobcats are seldom seen but widely distributed in the canyon.

BOBCAT
(*Lynx rufus*)

Description. Short-tailed, stocky, spotted cat, slightly larger than a house cat. Overall length up to thirty-three inches. Generally yellow-brown, lighter underneath. Black-tipped tail.

Distribution. Throughout park, often near rocky areas.

Remarks. Primarily eats small birds, rodents, rabbits, other small prey.

Deer Family

Deer have large eyes, are herbivorous, and are built for running. Male deer have antlers that they shed annually.

ELK
(Cervus elaphus)

Description. Large, reddish brown deer-like animal; weighs up to 750 pounds. Tawny butt patch. Large, spreading antlers in males.

Distribution. Forests on rims. Numbers are increasing.

Remarks. The native elk of region, Merriam's elk, was killed in such large numbers that it is extinct. The elk now in Grand Canyon region is Rocky Mountain elk, transplanted to region in 1913 and 1928. During autumn rut, bull bugles or makes shrill whistle to attract females and announce presence to other bulls.

Bull elk. The native elk were hunted to extinction. All elk seen in the park today are descendants of Rocky Mountain elk transplanted to the region earlier in the century.

Named for their large, mulelike ears, mule deer are distributed throughout the park but are most abundant on the South and North rims.

MULE DEER
(Odocoileus hemionus)

Description. Grayish brown deer with large, mulelike ears. Tail white, black-tipped. Large eyes. Up to six feet long. Males weigh up to 250 pounds.
Distribution. Primarily on rims, occasionally seen in canyon.
Remarks. Primarily eats shrubs, including sagebrush, cliffrose, aspen, other plants. Herd size varies significantly because of weather conditions, disease, predation, and other factors. Mountain lion is now well-established predator of Canyon deer.

Pronghorn Family

There is only one representative of this family, the pronghorn of North America. It is the only animal that annually sheds its horn sheaths, leaving behind a bony core. The horn is pronged, or forked, in mature bucks. The animal has been clocked at up to 70 miles per hour.

PRONGHORN ANTELOPE
(*Antilocapra americana*)

Description. Black, two-pronged horns fifteen to twenty inches long. Tan body with conspicuous white on rump and sides. White stripes across throat. Delicate features, large eyes.

Distribution. Open, flat areas. Formerly on South Rim, with occasional sightings over the years. Once abundant on flats south of canyon rim but never found inside canyon. Still live just south of park on Tusayan Ranger District by Ten X Campground and Red Butte.

Remarks. Sagebrush is major winter food. Once nearly as numerous as bison in West; hunting reduced pronghorns to a low of 20,000 by 1924. Numbers have risen to perhaps 800,000 throughout West.

Bovidae Family

These are hoofed mammals that include domestic cattle and sheep. They are primarily grassland dwellers. The only representative in the Grand Canyon is the bighorn sheep.

BIGHORN SHEEP
(*Ovis canadensis*)

Description. Tan, bulky, whitish belly and rump. Horns of male are large, amber, and curving. Females have smaller, knife-like amber horns.

Desert bighorn sheep live in the rugged parts of the canyon where they feed upon grasses and shrubs. Nearly extirpated by introduced diseases from domestic livestock, bighorns are making a slow comeback in the canyon.

Distribution. Rocky areas with cliffs or steep terrain nearby on both sides of canyon. Can be seen on South Rim, along the river, and elsewhere.

Remarks. Eats grass and browse. Uses cliffs to discourage predators, so is seldom far from steep terrain. In autumn, males engage in spirited head-battering duels to determine access to ewes for breeding purposes. Early Indian accounts suggest bighorn was once abundant in canyon, but diseases from domestic sheep grazing nearby killed many, not only in canyon but throughout West. Numbers have been increasing in recent years.

Attractions Beyond the Canyon

Hualapai Indian Reservation

Bordering the Colorado River for 108 miles, the Hualapai Reservation is located along the southwest boundary of Grand Canyon National Park. The 992,000-acre reservation is home to 900-plus Yuman-speaking tribe members. The Hualapai are descended from the Cerbat people, who appear to have moved into the Grand Canyon region about 1300 A.D. The river figures significantly in their spiritual mythology. They believe they were created from its mud and sand.

Navajo Indian Reservation

Along the eastern boundaries of Grand Canyon National Park lies the Navajo Indian Reservation. At 9 million acres, the reservation, three times the size of Connecticut, takes in the entire northeastern corner of Arizona, including such well-known sites as Monument Valley and Canyon de Chelly. The Navajo are recent residents of the Southwest, arriving from the north around 1500, or about the same date the Spanish penetrated New Mexico. Raiders and slave traders, the Navajo preyed on the other tribes like the Hopi, as well as Spanish settlements, until they were defeated by the U.S. Army and placed on this reservation. The Navajo have a number of sacred sites within the canyon, in particular salt deposits along the Little Colorado River.

Havasupai Indian Reservation

The 185,000-acre Havasupai Reservation is considered by many to be one of the most beautiful sections of the canyon, with waterfalls and lovely canyon walls. A visit to the Havasupai Reservation can be considered close to paradise. The tribe has rights to public lands for hunting, gathering, and livestock grazing, including Grand Canyon National Park. Red Butte, just to the south of Tusayan, is thought to be the birthplace of the Havasupai tribe. The Hance Trail into the canyon also has religious significance.

Although the Havasupai have always lived in Havasu Canyon, tribal members have lived elsewhere in the canyon. During the late 1800s, a few families lived at Indian Gardens and one resided below the Desert View area. During the 1920s and 1930s, a few Havasupai families lived around Grand Canyon Village while employed by concessionaires and the park. Descendants of these families still work in the park.

Kaibab National Forest

The 1,534,443 acres of what is today the Kaibab National Forest was set aside in 1893 as part of the Grand Canyon National Forest Reserve. In 1906, President Theodore Roosevelt created the Grand Canyon Game Preserve, which included much of what is now the national forest. In 1908, the area that included the game preserve was redesignated the Kaibab National Forest. In 1919, the lands making up today's national park were carved from the national forest. In 1934, the Tusayan National Forest, south of the canyon, was joined with Kaibab National Forest to create the general outline of the present Kaibab National Forest.

Today the forest is divided into four ranger districts. Elevations range from 3,000 to 10,418 feet. Unlike national parks, which preserve natural values, public amenities, and native species, national forests operate upon a policy euphemistically called "multiple use." Logging, grazing, and mining tend to have priority over other public concerns like wilderness recreation and protection of wildlife, watersheds, and soils. Recently, the overwhelming commercial emphasis has changed slightly to focus more on ecosystems, but industries have staunch local and some congressional support. Overall public benefits are still secondary to private commercial interests.

Two of the forest's four ranger districts border Grand Canyon National Park. The North District encompasses the northern portion of the Kaibab Plateau and is adjacent to the North Rim of the Grand Canyon. Beautiful forests of ponderosa, aspen, spruce, and fir cover much of the national forest. Camping is permitted. Hiking is limited, particularly in the ranger district's two designated wilderness areas, Kanab Creek and Saddle Mountain, described in detail below.

Outside of these rugged and unroaded enclaves, the Kaibab Ranger District has suffered extensively from logging and grazing. The extensive road network and loss of old-growth trees has hurt species like the Southwest spotted owl, Southwest goshawk, and many cavity-nesting birds that depend on the dead and dying snags of a healthy forest. Grazing removes forage that would support native species from butterflies to hummingbirds. Also, native predators like wolves have been killed to keep the plateau safe for domestic animals.

The Tusayan District takes in 360,000 acres and lies on the northern portion of the Coconino Plateau just south of the park. Much of the district is open sagebrush-grasslands mixed with patches of ponderosa. There are a number of campgrounds adjacent to or near the park as well as two trails. The Arizona Trail, which runs the length of the state, crosses part of the district.

The forest is home to a few larger mammals, including black bears, elk, antelope, mule deer, bobcats, mountain lions, and coyotes.

House Rock Valley Buffalo Ranch

In 1906, Charles "Buffalo" Jones brought a small herd of bison to the Kaibab Plateau. Eventually, the state acquired them and they were moved to House Rock Valley in 1926. Today, the 100 or so bison roam the same area under the management of the Arizona Game and Fish Department.

Wupatki National Monument

The 700-year-old Sinaguan and Anasazi ruins at Wupatki National Monument were abandoned about 1225. Dwellings at the site range from single-family houses to high-rises of up to 100 rooms. The monument was established in 1924 and covers fifty-six square miles. A paved loop drive off Highway 89 takes visitors by several ruins.

Sunset Crater National Monument

Sunset Crater features a prominent 1,000-foot cone of the Sunset Volcano, which erupted in 1064–65. Eruptions continued for 200 years, with the last major outburst in 1250. Sunset Crater was named by famed Grand Canyon explorer John Wesley Powell in 1885. To protect the area, it was designated as a national monument in 1930.

Sunset Crater, Sunset Crater National Monument. Sunset Crater last erupted in 1250.

Wilderness Areas

Wilderness areas are parcels of public land designated by Congress to be managed so as to retain their natural qualities. Timber cutting, mining, and motor vehicles are banned. Hiking, skiing, horseback riding, and other nonmechanized forms of transportation are allowed. Most Bureau of Land Management and national forest wildernesses permit hunting and fishing.

Kendrick Mountain Wilderness

The Kendrick Mountain Wilderness straddles the Coconino and Kaibab national forests. Part of the San Francisco Peaks volcanic field, Kendrick Mountain rises to 10,418 feet. The steep mountain is cloaked in forests of ponderosa, white and Douglas fir, and southwestern white pine. Meadows are abundant on the north and west slopes. Wildlife includes red squirrels, spotted owls, elk, goshawks, and pygmy nuthatches. A fire lookout is located on top of the mountain.

Kanab Creek Wilderness

The remote 75,300-acre Kanab Creek Wilderness is adjacent to the western edge of the Kaibab Plateau. The creek is in a tributary canyon on the north side of the Grand Canyon. The creek and its tributaries have carved deep gorges into the plateaus north of the river. Elevations are between 2,000 and 6,000 feet. The few trails in this region are poorly marked. Water is scarce. Bighorn sheep and the endangered peregrine falcon can be found in this area.

Saddle Mountain Wilderness

The Saddle Mountain Wilderness lies on the northeast edge of Grand Canyon National Park and along the eastern border of the Kaibab Plateau. Elevations vary between 6,000 and 8,000 feet. A fire in the 1960s spurred the regrowth of shrubs that have created ideal mule deer habitat. The area is also home to the rare Apache trout, an endangered species, and lies on the edge of the bison herd range in the House Rock Valley.

Ponderosa pines frame Kendrick Mountain Wilderness and the San Francisco Peaks in the Coconino National Forest.

Paria Canyon–Vermillion Cliffs Wilderness

The 112,000-acre Paria Canyon–Vermillion Cliffs Wilderness lies just north of Marble Canyon along the Utah-Arizona line. The cliffs, a 3,000-foot escarpment of Navajo sandstone, tower above Highway 89. Some of the best slot canyons in the Colorado Plateau are found here. Mule deer and desert bighorn sheep are found in the area. The wilderness was selected as a potential California condor reintroduction site.

Cottonwood Point Wilderness

The 6,860-acre Cottonwood Point Wilderness lies on the Utah line just north of Arizona Highway 389. It contains 1,000-foot cliffs of Navajo sandstone and small wooded canyons. Pinyon-juniper woodlands and sagebrush dominate the area.

Grand Wash Cliffs Wilderness

This 37,030-acre wilderness lies south of St. George, Utah, along the western boundary of Grand Canyon National Park. It protects a twelve-

Saddle Mountain Wilderness on the eastern border of the Kaibab National Forest is one of several wilderness areas adjoining the park on the Kaibab Plateau.

Sunset at Cape Royal, North Rim.

mile stretch of the Grand Wash Cliffs. Rugged canyons and a towering wall of cliffs mark the edge of the Colorado Plateau and beginning of the Basin and Range Province. This is an important area for desert tortoise and bighorn sheep.

Mount Trumbull Wilderness

This 7,880-acre wilderness lies just north of the Grand Canyon. Part of the Uinkaret Mountains, Mount Trumbull is a large basalt-capped mesa covered with a virgin ponderosa forest. Kaibab squirrels, wild turkeys, and mule deer are found in the area.

Mount Logan Wilderness

The 14,650-acre Mount Logan Wilderness is immediately adjacent to the Grand Canyon near the Toroweap Valley. Mount Logan consists of volcanic flows. The area is covered with ponderosa forests and is home to the Kaibab squirrel.

Mammal List

Abundance ratings are generalized. Some species, such as birds, bats, and other migratory species, are common only during breeding season or migration and may be rare otherwise. Some are common in certain habitats, such as along the river, but may be rare elsewhere. Some species' abundance may vary from year to year because of weather conditions or natural cycles. I did not include accidental species or creatures whose ranges should overlap the canyon but that have not been officially recorded.

Abundance Rating

C - *Common*. Abundant. Likely to be encountered in the appropriate habitat.

U - *Uncommon*. Infrequently seen.

R - *Rare*. Unlikely to be encountered, though within the normal range for the animal.

Ca - *Casual*. Outside the species' normal range, but occasionally reported.

Shrews
____ Merriam shrew
(*Sorex merriami*) (R)
____ Dwarf shrew
(*Sorex nanus*) (R)
____ Desert shrew
(*Notiosorex crawfordi*) (R)

Bats
____ Yuma myotis
(*Myotis yumanensis*) (C)

____ Long-eared myotis
(*Myotis evotis*) (U)
____ Fringe-tailed myotis
(*Myotis thysanodes*) (U)
____ Long-legged myotis
(*Myotis volans*) (C)
____ California myotis
(*Myotis californicus*) (C)
____ Small-footed myotis
(*Myotis leibii*) (U)

____ Silver-haired bat
(*Lasionycteris noctivagans*) (R)

____ Western pipistrelle
(*Pipistrellus hesperus*) (C)

____ Big brown bat
(*Eptesicus fuscus*) (C)

____ Red bat
(*Lasiurus borealis*) (R)

____ Hoary bat
(*Lasiurus cinereus*) (R)

____ Townsend's big-eared bat
(*Plecotus townsendii*) (U)

____ Mexican big-eared bat
(*Idionycteris phyllotis*) (Ca)

____ Pallid bat
(*Antrozous pallidus*) (C)

____ Mexican free-tailed bat
(*Tadarida brasiliensis*) (U)

____ Big free-tailed bat
(*Tadarida macrotis*) (R)

Hares and Rabbits

____ Black-tailed jackrabbit
(*Lepus californicus*) (U)

____ Mountain (Nuttall's)
cottontail
(*Sylvilagus nuttallii*) (U)

____ Desert cottontail
(*Sylvilagus auduboni*) (C)

Squirrels, Chipmunks, and Prairie Dogs

____ Gunnison's prairie dog
(*Cynomys gunnisoni*) (R)

____ Spotted ground squirrel
(*Spermophilus spilosoma*) (R)

____ Rock squirrel
(*Spermophilus variegatus*) (C)

____ Golden-mantled ground
squirrel
(*Spermophilus lateralis*) (C)

____ Harris antelope squirrel
(*Ammospermophilus harrisi*)
(R)

____ White-tailed antelope squirrel
(*Ammospermophilus leucurus*)
(C)

____ Least chipmunk
(*Eutamias minimus*) (C)

____ Uinta chipmunk
(*Eutamias umbrinus*) (C)

____ Cliff chipmunk
(*Eutamias dorsalis*) (C)

____ Abert squirrel
(*Sciurus aberti aberti*) (U)

____ Kaibab squirrel
(*Sciurus aberti kaibabensis*) (C)

____ Red squirrel
(*Tamiasciurus hudsonicus*) (C)

Pocket Gophers

____ Common pocket gopher
(*Thomomys bottae*) (C)

____ Northern pocket gopher
(*Thomomys talpoides*) (C)

Pocket Mice and Kangaroo Rats

____ Silky pocket mouse
(*Perognathus flavus*) (U)

____ Long-tailed pocket mouse
(*Perognathus formosus*) (U)

____ Rock pocket mouse
(*Perognathus intermedius*) (C)

____ Merriam kangaroo rat
(*Dipodomys merriami*) (R)

____ Ord's kangaroo rat
(*Dipodomys ordii*) (R)

Beavers
____ Beaver
(*Castor canadensis*) (U)

New World Rats and Mice
____ Western harvest mouse
(*Reithrodontomys megalotis*) (C)
____ Canyon mouse
(*Peromyscus crinitus*) (C)
____ Cactus mouse
(*Peromyscus eremicus*) (C)
____ Deer mouse
(*Peromyscus maniculatus*) (C)
____ Brush mouse
(*Peromyscus boylei*) (C)
____ Pinyon mouse
(*Peromyscus truei*) (C)
____ Northern grasshopper mouse
(*Onychomys leucogaster*) (U)
____ White-throated wood rat
(*Neotoma albigula*) (C)
____ Desert wood rat
(*Neotoma lepida*) (C)
____ Stephens wood rat
(*Neotoma stephensi*) (C)
____ Mexican wood rat
(*Neotoma mexicana*) (C)
____ Bushy-tailed wood rat
(*Neotoma cinerea*) (C)
____ Long-tailed vole
(*Microtus longicaudus*) (C)
____ Mexican vole
(*Microtus mexicanus*) (C)

American Porcupines
____ North American porcupine
(*Erethizon dorsatum*) (C)

Dog Family
____ Coyote
(*Canis latrans*) (C)
____ Gray fox
(*Urocyon cinereoargenteus*) (U)

Bears
____ Black bear
(*Ursus americanus*) (R)

Raccoon Family
____ Ringtail
(*Bassariscus astutus*) (C)
____ Raccoon
(*Procyon lotor*) (R)

Weasel Family
____ Long-tailed weasel
(*Mustela frenata*) (U)
____ American badger
(*Taxidea taxus*) (U)
____ Western spotted skunk
(*Spilogale putorius*) (C)
____ Striped skunk
(*Mephitis mephitis*) (C)
____ River otter
(*Lutra canadensis*) (R)

Cat Family
____ Mountain lion
(*Felis concolor*) (R)
____ Bobcat
(*Lynx rufus*) (C)

Deer Family

_____ Elk
    (Cervus elaphus) (R)
_____ Mule deer
    (Odocoileus hemionus) (C)

_____ Pronghorn antelope
    (Antilocapra americana) (R)
_____ Desert bighorn sheep
    (Ovis canadensis) (U)

Bird List

Abundance Rating

C - *Common*. Almost always seen in appropriate habitat.

U - *Uncommon*. Infrequently seen.

R - *Rare*. Little likelihood of encountering species in appropriate habitat, but not out of species' normal range.

I - *Irregular*. Found only occasionally a few times a decade.

A - *Accidental*. Far out of species' range and not expected to be seen again.

Ca - *Casual*. Out of species' normal range, but may be seen again.

Loons

_____ Common loon
   (*Gavia immer*) (Ca)

Grebes

_____ Pied-billed grebe
   (*Podilymbus podiceps*) (R)

_____ Eared grebe
   (*Podiceps nigricollis*) (U)

_____ Western grebe
   (*Aechmophorus occidentalis*) (R)
   (common on upper portion of
   Lake Mead)

Pelicans

_____ White pelican
   (*Pelecanus erythrorynchos*) (R)

_____ Brown pelican
   (*Pelecanus occidentalis*) (Ca)

Cormorants

_____ Double-crested cormorant
   (*Phalacrocorax auritus*) (U)

Herons

_____ Great blue heron
   (*Ardea herodias*) (C)

_____ Great egret
   (*Casmerodius albus*) (R)

_____ Snowy egret
   (*Egretta thula*) (U)

_____ Green-backed heron
   (*Butorides striatus*) (R)

_____ Black-crowned night heron
   (*Nycticorax nycticorax*) (U)

Ibis

_____ White-faced ibis
   (*Plegadis chihi*) (U)

Geese and Ducks

____ Canada goose
(*Branta canadensis*) (C)

____ Green-winged teal
(*Anas crecca*) (U)

____ Mallard
(*Anas platyrhynchos*) (C)

____ Northern pintail
(*Anas acuta*) (U)

____ Blue-winged teal
(*Anas discors*) (C)

____ Cinnamon teal
(*Anas cyanoptera*) (U)

____ Northern shoveler
(*Anas clypeata*) (R)

____ Gadwall
(*Anas strepera*) (C)

____ American wigeon
(*Anas americana*) (C)

____ Canvasback
(*Aythya valisineria*) (R)

____ Redhead
(*Aythya americana*) (R)

____ Ring-necked duck
(*Aythya collaris*) (R)

____ Lesser scaup
(*Aythya affinis*) (C)

____ Common goldeneye
(*Bucephala clangula*) (U)

____ Bufflehead
(*Bucephala albeola*) (C)

____ Common merganser
(*Mergus merganser*) (C)

____ Ruddy duck
(*Oxyura jamaicensis*) (R)

Vultures

____ Turkey vulture
(*Cathartes aura*) (C)

Eagles and Hawks

____ Osprey
(*Pandion haliaetus*) (U)

____ Bald eagle
(*Haliaeetus leucocephalus*) (C)

____ Northern harrier
(*Circus cyaneus*) (U)

____ Sharp-shinned hawk
(*Accipiter striatus*) (U)

____ Cooper's hawk
(*Accipiter cooperii*) (U)

____ Northern goshawk
(*Accipiter gentilis*) (U)

____ Swainson's hawk
(*Buteo swainsoni*) (U)

____ Red-tailed hawk
(*Buteo jamaicensis*) (C)

____ Ferruginous hawk
(*Buteo regalis*) (U)

____ Rough-legged hawk
(*Buteo lagopus*) (U)

____ Golden eagle
(*Aquila chrysaetos*) (U)

Falcons

____ American kestrel
(*Falco sparverius*) (C)

____ Merlin
(*Falco columbarius*) (I)

____ Peregrine falcon
(*Falco peregrinus*) (C)

____ Prairie falcon
(*Falco mexicanus*) (R)

Grouse Family

____ Chukar
(*Alectoris chukar*) (U)

____ Blue grouse
(*Dendragapus obscurus*) (U)

_____ Wild turkey
(*Meleagris gallopavo*) (C)
_____ Gambel's quail
(*Lophortyx gambelii*) (C)

Rails
_____ American coot
(*Fulica americana*) (C)

Plovers
_____ Killdeer
(*Charadrius vociferus*) (U)

Stilts and Avocets
_____ Black-necked stilt
(*Himantopus mexicanus*) (U)
_____ American avocet
(*Recurvirostra americana*) (U)

Sandpipers and Phalaropes
_____ Greater yellowlegs
(*Tringa flavipes*) (R)
_____ Solitary sandpiper
(*Tringa solitaria*) (U)
_____ Willet
(*Catoptrophorus semipalmatus*)
(U)
_____ Spotted sandpiper
(*Actitis macularia*) (C)
_____ Western sandpiper
(*Calidris mauri*) (R)
_____ Common snipe
(*Gallinago gallinago*) (U)
_____ Wilson's phalarope
(*Phalaropus tricolor*) (R)
_____ Red-necked phalarope
(*Phalaropus lobatus*) (R)

Gulls and Terns
_____ Ring-billed gull
(*Larus delawarensis*) (U)
_____ California gull
(*Larus californicus*) (U)

Pigeons and Doves
_____ Band-tailed pigeon
(*Columba fasciata*) (U)
_____ Mourning dove
(*Zenaida macroura*) (C)

Roadrunners
_____ Greater roadrunner
(*Geococcyx californianus*) (U)

Owls
_____ Flammulated owl
(*Otus flammeolus*) (C)
_____ Western screech owl
(*Otus kennicottii*) (U)
_____ Great horned owl
(*Bubo virginianus*) (C)
_____ Northern pygmy owl
(*Glaucidium gnoma*) (R)
_____ Spotted owl
(*Strix occidentalis*) (R)
_____ Long-eared owl
(*Asio otus*) (U)

Goatsuckers
_____ Lesser nighthawk
(*Chordeiles acutipennis*) (R)
_____ Common nighthawk
(*Chordeiles minor*) (C)
_____ Common poorwill
(*Phalaenoptilus nuttallii*) (C)

Swifts
____ White-throated swift
(*Aeronautes saxatalis*)

Hummingbirds
____ Magnificent hummingbird
(*Eugenes fulgens*) (R)
____ Black-chinned hummingbird
(*Archilochus alexandri*) (C)
____ Costa's hummingbird
(*Calypte costae*) (C)
____ Calliope hummingbird
(*Stellula calliope*) (U)
____ Broad-tailed hummingbird
(*Selasphorus platycercus*) (C)
____ Rufous hummingbird
(*Selasphorus rufus*) (C)

Kingfishers
____ Belted kingfisher
(*Ceryle alcyon*) (C)

Woodpeckers
____ Lewis's woodpecker
(*Melanerpes lewis*) (U)
____ Acorn woodpecker
(*Melanerpes formicivorus*) (U)
____ Williamson's sapsucker
(*Sphyrapicus thyroideus*) (U)
____ Ladder-backed woodpecker
(*Picoides scalaris*) (R)
____ Downy woodpecker
(*Picoides pubescens*) (R)
____ Red-naped sapsucker
(*Sphyrapicus nuchalis*) (C)
____ Hairy woodpecker
(*Picoides villosus*) (C)

____ Three-toed woodpecker
(*Picoides tridactylus*) (R)
____ Northern flicker
(*Colaptes auratus*) (C)

Flycatchers
____ Olive-sided flycatcher
(*Contopus borealis*) (U)
____ Western wood-pewee
(*Contopus sordidulus*) (C)
____ Willow flycatcher
(*Empidonax traillii*) (R)
____ Gray flycatcher
(*Empidonax wrightii*) (C)
____ Black phoebe
(*Sayornis nigricans*) (C)
____ Say's phoebe
(*Sayornis saya*) (C)
____ Ash-throated flycatcher
(*Myiarchus cinerascens*) (C)
____ Cassin's kingbird
(*Tyrannus vociferans*) (C)
____ Western kingbird
(*Tyrannus verticalis*) (U)

Larks
____ Horned lark
(*Eremophila alpestris*) (C)

Swallows
____ Purple martin
(*Progne subis*) (U)
____ Northern rough-winged
swallow
(*Stelgidopteryx serripennis*) (C)
____ Violet-green swallow
(*Tachycineta thalassina*) (C)

Jays and Crows
____ Steller's jay
(*Cyanocitta stelleri*) (C)
____ Scrub jay
(*Aphelocoma coerulescens*) (C)
____ Pinyon jay
(*Gymnorhinus cyanocephalus*)
(C)
____ Clark's nutcracker
(*Nucifraga columbiana*) (C)
____ Common raven
(*Corvus corax*) (C)

Titmice
____ Mountain chickadee
(*Parus gambeli*) (C)
____ Plain titmouse
(*Parus inornatus*) (C)

Bushtits
____ Bushtit
(*Psaltriparus minimus*) (C)

Nuthatches
____ Red-breasted nuthatch
(*Sitta canadensis*) (U)
____ White-breasted nuthatch
(*Sitta carolinensis*) (C)
____ Pygmy nuthatch
(*Sitta pygmaea*) (C)

Creepers
____ Brown creeper
(*Certhia americana*) (C)

Wrens
____ Rock wren
(*Salpinctes obsoletus*) (C)

____ Canyon wren
(*Catherpes mexicanus*) (C)
____ Bewick wren
(*Thryomanes bewickii*) (C)
____ House wren
(*Troglodytes aedon*) (C)
____ Winter wren
(*Troglodytes troglodytes*) (R)

Dippers
____ American dipper
(*Cinclus mexicanus*) (C)

Kinglets, Thrushes, and Solitaires
____ Golden-crowned kinglet
(*Regulus satrapa*) (U)
____ Ruby-crowned kinglet
(*Regulus calendula*) (C)
____ Blue-gray gnatcatcher
(*Polioptila caerulea*) (C)
____ Western bluebird
(*Sialia mexicana*) (C)
____ Mountain bluebird
(*Sialia currucoides*) (C)
____ Townsend's solitaire
(*Myadestes townsendi*) (C)
____ Hermit thrush
(*Catharus guttatus*) (C)
____ American robin
(*Turdus migratorius*) (C)

Mockingbirds and Thrashers
____ Northern mockingbird
(*Mimus polyglottos*) (U)
____ Sage thrasher
(*Oreoscoptes montanus*) (U)

Silky Flycatchers

_____ Phainopepla
(*Phainopepla nitens*) (U)

Shrikes

_____ Loggerhead shrike
(*Lanius ludovicianus*) (U)

Starlings

_____ European starling
(*Sturnus vulgaris*) (U)

Vireos

_____ Bell's vireo
(*Vireo bellii*) (C)
_____ Gray vireo
(*Vireo vicinior*) (U)
_____ Solitary vireo
(*Vireo solitarius*) (C)
_____ Warbling vireo
(*Vireo gilvus*) (C)

Warblers

_____ Orange-crowned warbler
(*Vermivora celata*) (U)
_____ Nashville warbler
(*Vermivora ruficapilla*) (U)
_____ Virginia's warbler
(*Vermivora virginiae*) (C)
_____ Lucy's warbler
(*Vermivora luciae*) (C)
_____ Yellow warbler
(*Dendroica petechia*) (C)
_____ Yellow-rumped warbler
(*Dendroica coronata*) (C)
_____ Black-throated gray warbler
(*Dendroica nigrescens*) (C)
_____ Hermit warbler

(*Dendroica occidentalis*) (U)
_____ Grace's warbler
(*Dendroica graciae*) (C)
_____ MacGillivray's warbler
(*Oporornis tolmiei*) (U)
_____ Common yellowthroat
(*Geothlypis trichas*) (C)
_____ Wilson's warbler
(*Wilsonia pusilla*) (C)
_____ Red-faced warbler
(*Cardellina rubrifrons*) (C)
_____ Yellow-breasted chat
(*Icteria virens*) (C)

Tanagers

_____ Summer tanager
(*Piranga rubra*) (R)
_____ Western tanager
(*Piranga ludoviciana*) (C)

Grosbeaks and Allies

_____ Black-headed grosbeak
(*Pheucticus melanocephalus*)
(C)
_____ Blue grosbeak
(*Guiraca caerulea*) (C)
_____ Lazuli bunting
(*Passerina amoena*) (C)

Towhees, Sparrows, and Juncos

_____ Green-tailed towhee
(*Pipilo chlorurus*) (C)
_____ Rufous-sided towhee
(*Pipilo erythrophthalmus*) (C)
_____ Chipping sparrow
(*Spizella passerina*) (C)
_____ Lark sparrow
(*Chondestes grammacus*) (U)

____ Black-throated sparrow
(*Amphispiza bilineata*) (C)
____ Song sparrow
(*Melospiza melodia*) (U)
____ White-crowned sparrow
(*Zonotrichia leucophrys*) (C)
____ Dark-eyed junco
(*Junco hyemalis*) (C)

Blackbirds and Orioles
____ Red-winged blackbird
(*Agelaius phoeniceus*) (U)
____ Western meadowlark
(*Sturnella neglecta*) (C)
____ Brewer's blackbird
(*Euphagus cyanocephalus*) (C)
____ Great-tailed grackle
(*Quiscalus mexicanus*) (C)
____ Brown-headed cowbird
(*Molothrus ater*) (C)

____ Hooded oriole
(*Icterus cucullatus*) (C)
____ Bullock's oriole
(*Icterus galbula*) (U)
____ Scott's Oriole
(*Icterus parisorum*) (U)

Finches and Allies
____ Cassin's finch
(*Carpodacus cassinii*) (U)
____ Pine siskin
(*Carduelis pinus*) (C)
____ Lesser goldfinch
(*Carduelis psaltria*) (C)

Old World Sparrows
____ House sparrow
(*Passer domesticus*) (C)

AMPHIBIAN AND REPTILE LIST

Abundance Rating

C - *Common.* Abundant. Likely to be encountered in the appropriate habitat.

U - *Uncommon.* Infrequently seen.

R - *Rare.* Unlikely to be encountered, though within the normal range for the animal.

Ca - *Casual.* Outside the species' normal range, but occasionally reported.

Mole Salamanders

____ Utah tiger salamander
(*Ambystoma tigrinum utahensis*)
(C) (Adults uncommon)

____ Arizona tiger salamander
(*Ambystoma tigrinum nebulosum*) (R)

True Toads

____ Rocky Mountain toad
(*Bufo woodhousei woodhousei*)
(C)

____ Red-spotted toad
(*Bufo punctatus*) (C)

Spadefoot Toads

____ Great Basin spadefoot toad
(*Scaphiopus intermontanus*) (C)

Tree Frogs

____ Canyon tree frog
(*Hyla arenicolor*) (C)

True Frogs

____ Leopard frog
(*Rana pipiens*) (R)

Geckos

____ Desert banded gecko
(*Coleonyx variegatus variegatus*)
(C)

Night Lizards

____ Arizona night lizard
(*Xantusia vigilis arizonae*) (R)

Iguanid Lizards

____ Western chuckwalla
(*Sauromalus obesus obesus*) (U)

____ Zebra-tailed lizard
(*Callisaurus draconoides*) (U)

____ Long-nosed leopard lizard
(*Gambelia wislizenii*) (R)

____ Collared lizard
(*Crotaphytus collaris baileyi*)
(C)

____ Mojave black-collared lizard
(*Crotaphytus insularis
bicinctores*) (C)

____ Yellow-backed spiny lizard
(*Sceloporus magister uniformis*)
(C)

____ Northern plateau lizard
(*Sceloporus undulatus elongatus*) (C)

____ Southern plateau lizard
(*Sceloporus undulatus tristichus*)
(C)

____ Northern sagebrush lizard
(*Sceloporus graciosus graciosus*)
(C)

____ Tree lizard
(*Urosaurus ornatus*) (C)

____ Desert side-blotched lizard
(*Uta stansburiana stejnegeri*)
(C)

____ Northern side-blotched lizard
(*Uta stansburiana stansburiana*)
(C)

____ Mountain short-horned lizard
(*Phrynosoma douglasii
hernandesi*) (C)

____ Southern desert horned lizard
(*Phrynosoma platyrhinos
calidiarum*) (R)

Whiptails

____ Northern whiptail
(*Cnemidophorus tigris
septentrionalis*) (C)

Skinks

____ Southern many-lined skink
(*Eumeces multivirgatus
epipleurotus*) (R)

____ Great Basin skink
(*Eumeces skiltonianus
utahensis*) (R)

Gila Monsters

____ Banded Gila monster
(*Heloderma suspectum cinctum*)
(R)

Blind Snakes

____ Western blind snake
(*Leptotyphlops humilis*) (R)

Common Harmless Snakes

____ Red racer snake
(*Masticophis flagellum*) (U)

____ Desert striped whipsnake
(*Masticophis taeniatus
taeniatus*) (C)

____ Mojave patch-nosed snake
(*Salvadora hexalepis
mojavensis*) (U)

____ Sonoran lyre snake
(*Trimorphodon biscutatus
lambda*) (R)

____ Sonoran gopher snake
(*Pituophis melanoleucus affinis*)
(C)

____ Great Basin gopher snake
(*Pituophis melanoleucus deserticola*) (C)

____ Utah mountain king snake
(*Lampropeltis pyromelana infralabialis*) (R)

____ California mountain king snake
(*Lampropeltis getulus*) (C)

____ Western long-nosed snake
(*Rhinocheilus lecontei lecontei*) (R)

____ Wandering garter snake
(*Thamnophis elegans vagrans*) (U)

____ Western ground snake
(*Sonora semiannulata gloydi*) (U)

____ Desert night snake
(*Hypsiglena torquata deserticola*) (R)

____ Spotted night snake
(*Hypsiglena torquata ochrorhynchus*) (R)

____ Utah black-headed snake
(*Tantilla planiceps*) (R)

Pit Vipers

____ Southwestern speckled rattlesnake
(*Crotalus mitchellii pyrrhus*) (R)

____ Northern black-tailed rattlesnake
(*Crotalus molossus molossus*) (R)

____ Grand Canyon rattlesnake
(*Crotalus viridis abyssus*) (U)

____ Great Basin rattlesnake
(*Crotalus viridis lutosus*) (U)

____ Hopi rattlesnake
(*Crotalus viridis nuntius*) (U)

FISH LIST

Native Fish

_____ Humpback chub
(Gila cypha)
_____ Speckled dace
(Rhinichthys osculus)
_____ Razorback sucker
(Xyrauchen texanus)
_____ Flannelmouth sucker
(Catostomus latipinnis)
_____ Bluehead sucker
(Catostomus discobolus)
_____ Roundtail chub
(Gila robusta)
_____ Bonytail chub
(Gila elegans)
_____ Colorado squawfish
(Ptychocheilus lucius)

Non-Native Introduced Species

_____ Rainbow trout
(Oncorhynchus mykiss)
_____ Brown trout
(Salmo trutta)
_____ Brook trout
(Salvelinus fontinalis)
_____ Carp
(Cyprinus carpio)
_____ Channel catfish
(Ictalurus punctatus)
_____ Fathead minnow
(Pimephales promelas)
_____ Rio Grande killifish
(Fundulus zebrinus)
_____ Striped bass
(Morone saxatilis)

Visitation Chart

	1994 Monthly Visitation	Rank by Total Number per Month
January	149,601	12
February	260,146	9
March	384,827	6
April	346,027	8
May	465,027	5
June	572,688	3
July	735,951	1
August	704,058	2
September	477,800	4
October	375,090	7
November	210,345	10
December	168,375	11

INDEX